Success in 30 Seconds

Discover the Secrets of a Winning First Impression

Seana

Aberon Publications
New York, NY

Success in 30 Seconds

ISBN# 978-0-9641959-0-5

Cover designed by Jonathan Gullery
Illustrations by Monikhaa

Acknowledgments

To my special assistants Hester Betlem, Jessica Kornberg, and Zach van Schouwen, I give my heartfelt thanks. For sharing all of their knowledge and support, I would like to thank Gerrie Pinckney, Carolyn Gustafson, Doris Pooser, Jean Patton, Hilka Kleinkenbery, Lisa Cunningham, and Bernice Kentner. I would also like to thank Gail Kump and Ian Kimmich for their support and efforts, as well as the many people who helped to make this book possible in so many little ways.

This book is dedicated to my children, Traciana and Michael Graves,
who always inspire me.

Success in 30 Seconds

Discover the Secrets of a Winning First Impression

CONTENTS

Preface

At any given time, any 30 seconds may be the most important half minute of your life. First impressions are often formed within 30 seconds and are usually hard to change afterward. Success or failure hinges on these initial perceptions. A successful first impression can unlock the door to personal, professional, and financial success. In today's fast-paced, competitive world, it is important to stand out from the crowd. Those who make the best first impressions in the least amount of time will beat out the competition in the business and social world.

In recent years, hundreds of thousands of jobs have been eliminated. Due to cutbacks in the job market and corporate outsourcing, more people are seeking the same jobs and vying for a shrinking pool of choice positions. In the coming years, the most desirable jobs will be even less available.

Competition is fierce on all levels and in all areas today, and this will likely increase.

Large companies can no longer be relied upon for stable, long-term employment and economic prosperity. Many corporations have closed manufacturing plants and offices. Cuts on all levels have caused a tremendous strain on the job market. High school and college graduates are finding it increasingly difficult to get work, and salespeople are competing for the same dollars.

Additionally, a significant number of adults are single today. Activities geared toward this group are always increasing, and the number of organizations whose services cater specifically to singles continues to grow. More personal ads are being used to connect socially. Dating services are popular. For better or worse, many social introductions are now made through videos and over the Internet. First impressions have therefore taken on greater importance than ever before, socially, professionally, and financially. By understanding what goes into making these impressions, you can learn how to present yourself as strongly and successfully as possible.

Part I

Polishing Your Presence

1

Success Starts with Your First Impression

The right first impression can help you to land that plum job, attract a significant other, win that sought after promotion, project a successful image, and increase your sales. Every day of your life, all day long, you are continually making first impressions. On many of these occasions, your success and happiness can hinge on those impressions.

As the term implies, first impressions are based on the image that you initially project. People begin to evaluate you and usually form lasting opinions of you from the very first moment that they meet you. You do the same with other people. Your first impression can inspire confidence in you and help people to see the unlimited potential in you.

Did you ever wish that you could "have a second chance to make a great first impression?" How many times have you wistfully thought this or said this? Think of the many times that you have replayed first meetings over and over again in your mind. Have you ever had occasion to say the following?:

"I wish I had said . . ."

"I wish I had done . . ."

"I wish I had worn . . ."

Your first impression can attract people to you or turn people away from you. It does not matter how wonderful you are or how much you know if no one is willing to take the time to find out. When people respond well to you initially, it increases your confidence, and a confident person becomes a more attractive and appealing person. This creates a kind of snowballing effect, with your first impression acting to start the ball rolling.

Whether or not you are aware of it, you are constantly marketing, promoting, and selling yourself—every day, all day long. This might happen while seeking a new job or promotion, meeting your future in-laws, going on that special first date, or attending your child's school play or a casual get-together. You are basically telling a story about yourself—a story about your personality, grooming, hygiene, diet, motivation, self-esteem, attitudes, and sense of style and color—your general identity. This evaluation takes place immediately and is reflected in your motions, your general appearance, and your facial expressions.

There is a definite connection between how you present yourself and how you are perceived. Initially, when you meet people, you are projecting a particular impression or perception of yourself; at the moment of first contact, the perception usually becomes the reality. This perception is based on what is initially or immediately perceived. People are so affected by this impression that it influences them even before they hear what you have to say or determine how much you know.

Many people react initially to what they see, followed by what they hear, and then by what they touch. That is why it is most important to make sure that what people initially perceive about you is exactly what you want to project. First impressions are formed on a subconscious level—that is, the person evaluating you is not consciously aware of what is happening—and are hard to change. To say that this first impression is formed within 30 seconds is a generous estimate. Years ago, it was thought that first impressions were formed within four minutes. Later, this was reduced to one minute. In today's fast-paced, fast-moving world, first impressions are often formed within a few seconds.

Before you can comfortably sell a product or a service, you have to sell yourself. This means being confident. Looking good and feeling good gives you confidence in yourself. A confident you inspires the confidence of others in you, thereby attracting social, professional, and financial success. People usually buy into an individual before they buy into business or social situations. People like to be involved with individuals to whom they have a positive reaction and with whom they feel comfortable, and this approval usually starts with a good first impression or positive image.

A store clerk's initial tone or manner may cause you to avoid shopping there in the future. The merchandise may be satisfactory but the attitude of this employee has left much to be desired. You do not complain to the management;

you simply choose not to shop at this store in the future.

You may stop at a restaurant for a cup of coffee and may consider having dinner there. Sometimes, the feel of the restaurant just turns you off (whether you perceive dirty tabletops, offensive odors or indifferent service). Often, it is just a *feeling* about the whole place that you do not like. On the other hand, a favorable impression could influence you to linger and to even return on other occasions.

These familiar experiences provide you with a hint of how you are perceived and judged in everyday situations. There may have been times when you have cold-called a business about a service or product. What you read from the voice of the employee can give you a positive or negative impression of that business, and this can affect your desire to do business with that company. Even if the manager or CEO of a company projects a positive image, this image must filter down to all levels of the company. A business is only as strong as all of the people who represent it—the whole organization.

Those who make the best first impression will be selected from among the rest and placed as front-runners. It will be more important than ever to put your best foot forward immediately. Spending time, energy, and money on your self-development and enhancement is one of the best investments that you can make.

Remember, you are unique; capitalize on this and make the most of it. Putting your best foot forward is not a hit-or-miss situation. There is a science to everything, including making a positive first impression. Personalize this science to fit your needs. That is what this book offers you—the particular know-how needed to help you achieve that all-important, positive first impression.

With the right first impression, you too, can begin to realize unlimited social, professional, and financial success. Good luck with your 30 seconds! Make your first impression count!

2

What's in a Color?

Color Yourself Confident and Attractive

The right choice of colors in your wardrobe and accessories is the starting point for every attractive and confident image. You may ask, "What does color really do for me?"

- Color is the first thing that people notice about you.
- It influences people's first impressions of you.
- Colors can completely change your appearance.
- Color affects how others think and feel about you.
- It affects your feelings and thoughts.

Color, then, plays a great role in helping you to put your best foot forward and give you the winning edge when you need it.

Have you ever gone to work after a long, restful night's sleep, energetic and ready to go, only to have people ask you all day long if you are feeling all right? "You look a little tired and drained today," someone might remark. By the end of the day, you are beginning to believe it yourself.

On the other hand, you have probably had the phone ring in the middle of the night only to find it was a wrong number. Afterward, you were unable to go back to sleep. After tossing and turning the rest of the night, you dragged yourself out of bed in the morning, just counting the hours until you could go back to bed. All day long, however, people complimented you on how terrific and rested you looked, even suggesting that you must have slept for 12 hours! Chances are the colors that you were wearing on these occasions had a lot to do with their responses.

Colors have tremendous power, and it is important to know how colors affect your appearance:

The Right Colors Can . . .	**The Wrong Colors Can . . .**
• diminish lines and wrinkles	• highlight lines and wrinkles
• make you appear alert and well-rested	• make you appear drained and tired
• make you look vibrant and energetic	• make you look washed out and lacking in enthusiasm
• create a healthy look	• give you a sallow, pale appearance

The Right Colors Can . . .

- create a positive mood around you
- attract people to you
- diminish dark circles
- make you appear younger
- soften your look
- even out your skin tone and flatter your complexion
- make you appear powerful and respected
- define and flatter your features
- help make you appear confident and at ease
- flatter your figure and make you appear slimmer
- add brightness and sparkle to your eyes
- help you to make a terrific first impression

The Wrong Colors Can . . .

- create a negative mood around you
- turn people off
- emphasize dark circles
- make you appear older
- give you a "hard" look
- cause your skin tone to appear uneven and blotchy
- make you appear weak and ineffectual
- blunt your features
- make you appear listless and drained
- make you look overweight or heavier
- give your eyes a dull, empty look
- spoil your first impression

Ellen was highly respected as the office manager of her company. When the company went out of business six months ago, she was sure that she would find another job right away. She was given excellent references. Much to her surprise, she is still unemployed. Needless to say, Ellen is very frustrated.

She has excellent skills and she is always pleasant. She is well groomed. She wears smart-looking business suits to her interviews. However, she chooses colors that overpower her and make her fade into the background. Even though she makes a point of going to bed early the night before an interview, she always looks tired and drained. She does not appear to be energetic and alert. No one wants to take a chance on hiring her.

Barbara, on the other hand, is a working mother and part-time student. Even when she is tired, she manages to look vibrant and well-rested. When she was in college, she attended a color analysis workshop. She learned what colors were the most flattering for her. She also learned what colors to eliminate from her wardrobe.

When she is making a presentation or if she has an important meeting to attend, she carefully chooses her best colors on those days. She looks attractive and confident. Barbara always makes a very positive impression. She has received several promotions and she expects to continue her advancement.

The right colors for your friend or significant other may be the wrong colors for you. Gerri Pinckney, author of *New Images for Women*, emphasized that you can probably wear quite a few different colors and look acceptable. However, you will look truly wonderful in those colors that are "just right" for you. Some people come alive in clear, crisp, vivid colors; softer, more muted colors may be more flattering to others. Most people will find a particular range of colors that suits them best.

Color should be wisely selected because it is so important. Make the most of it. People you meet should concentrate on you and not on what you are wearing. Do not choose colors in your clothes that will overpower you. A compliment should be directed to you and not your choice of apparel.

When you look great in what you are wearing, you usually feel great as well. You would not knowingly buy or wear clothes that make you look unattractive and unappealing, but a number of people make this mistake when they wear colors that cause this reaction. Avoid colors that fight each other or that are too busy for you.

The Characteristics of Color

The three primary colors are red, yellow, and blue. The combination of these colors produce all other colors. Colors are grouped according to value, undertone, and chroma or clarity. You will be able to wear quite a variety of colors, as long as you choose colors with the right characteristics. Familiarize yourself with these terms and understand them:

- Hue identifies a particular color, such as red or green.
- Value indicates the amount of lightness or darkness of a color, such as light green or dark green.
- Chroma or clarity relates to the brightness or dullness of a color; it can be clear (as in bright red) or muted (as in dull maroon).
- Undertone refers to how warm or cool a color is according to its blue or

yellow content, e.g. blue-green or yellow-green.

Know Your Colors

- Neutral colors form the basis of any good core wardrobe. They allow for versatility and endure with time.
- Basic colors are deeper in color than neutrals, but they are also a good choice when building a wardrobe. They can extend your wardrobe and make it more interesting.
- Bright colors make wonderful accent pieces when you want a touch or splash of color for a suit, coat, or dress in a neutral or basic color. They also work well in prints and stripes, especially in scarves or ties.
- Light colors provide flattering, pale touches near your face. They are great choices in blouses or shirts.

Note: All of these colors have warm or cool undertones. Bright colors are more popular today, and more people are wearing a wide range of colors. Just make sure that these colors are flattering and that you don't fade into the background.

What Determines Your Best Colors

Your skin, eye, and hair colors determine your best colors, and your heredity, in turn, determines your skin, eyes, and hair. When it comes to selecting the colors that are best for you, individual skin tone is the dominant factor.

Skin is made up of different hues. While it varies from individual to individual, it will fall within a certain range. Your skin will be either predominantly warm (yellow) or cool (blue) in undertone. Your hair and eyes will complement and blend with your skin tone. While there are different shades combined in your natural hair and eye pattern, they will always blend.

How to Determine Your Best Colors

Evaluating the right colors for you, based on your skin, hair, and eye pattern is called color analysis, and it's one of the best investments that you can make in yourself. Professional color analysts are available for this service, but choose one carefully: You want to know that he or she has had *extensive* training and experience. It takes time to develop this skill, and people often complain that they have been analyzed differently by different people. Ask these professionals beforehand about their training, background, work history, and number of years in the field. Also ask if they would be willing to supply references.

You can determine your basic color information by doing the following:

1. Find a place with as much natural light as possible, preferably near a window. Avoid fluorescent or artificial lighting, if possible.
2. Put on a white blouse or shirt. You may also use a white towel or sheet over your current outfit. This will help to avoid the distraction of one color against another. Mixing colors can make it difficult to be objective about various colors.
3. Shave if needed, and cleanse your skin of all makeup. Remove glasses or jewelry. They may reflect color or influence your color judgment.
4. Wrap a white towel around your head or use a shower cap if the natural

color of your hair has been changed at all.

5. Using a large mirror, determine different colors' effects on you. Start with colors already in your wardrobe: Try to determine which colors look the best. You will find a pattern emerging; you will look best in warmer tones rather than the cooler tones, or vice versa. Remember, you will generally look better in a particular range of colors. Do not be influenced by colors you have previously worn a lot or like very much.
6. Try to evaluate objectively the effect that certain colors have on you. Which look best on you? Which do not?
7. It would be helpful to have at least two people help you decide, as one person might not be objective enough. Someone else's choices are not necessarily right for you; they are usually influenced by their own preferences. (This is why using a professional color analyst is such a good investment!)

Another method for determining basic color differences and their effect on you involves the use of two sheets of white paper. Hold them under your hand or your arm. See what is reflected back to you—either a warm, yellow, peachy undertone or a cool, pinkish, blue undertone. The same test may be done with gold or silver jewelry.

Some people will look wonderful in both warm and cool colors, but most people will look best in one or the other. Review the effects of colors and see how these apply to you. For example, does the color you are evaluating make you look tired and sallow or rested and glowing?

Once you have determined what colors are best for you using analysis and trial and error, you are now ready to move forward. If you find that your existing wardrobe has predominantly fewer items with flattering colors for you, do not despair: Use what you have until you are able to make changes, which, for most people, will be gradual. Invest in one or two terrific shirts, blouses or scarves in great colors for you. This will offset the less flattering colors that you have been wearing.

The colors in your clothing and accessories should harmonize with the colors in your hair, makeup, and glasses. If you color your hair, use colors that support the colors in your clothing and accessories as well as your skin tone and eye color. This will create overall harmony. If you are not familiar with the right colors for your hair, seek help from a professional.

Color Analysis Methods

It will be of great help to you if you are familiar with the more widely used color analysis methods. Such familiarity will make you more knowledgeable when you consult a color analyst.

<u>Warm vs. Cool Method</u>

The easiest and most widely used system of color analysis is that based on the warm vs. cool concept. This system is increasingly being used by a number of cosmetic companies for coding cosmetics. It differentiates between warm and cool products—i.e., items with yellow-based undertones vs. blue-based undertones. For someone just starting out, this system is easiest to understand. It is a good starting place and can help you become more familiar with the basics of color analysis.

Seasonal Approach Method

Color analysis is also done according to the four seasons: winter, spring, summer, and autumn. While this is not a new method, it has become widely accepted and popular due to Carole Jackson's *Color Me Beautiful.* In this method, colors are grouped as follows:

- Winter—cool, clear—blue undertones
- Summer—cool, muted—blue undertones
- Spring—warm, clear—yellow undertones
- Autumn—warm, muted—yellow undertones

Color Analysis for Ethnic Skin Tones

This is a system of color analysis created by Jean Patton in *Color to Color: The Black Woman's Guide to a Rainbow of Fashion and Beauty.* She has created a system of color analysis that focuses on specific and unique complexion variations that exist among people of African, Latin, Asian, and Middle Eastern descents. Patton's approach to color analysis establishes principles that fit into four categories:

1. Warm colors
2. Cool colors
3. Warm and cool color variations
4. Balance of warm/cool colors

How Colors Affect You

Different colors evoke different feelings. Here are some basic colors and some of the more important thoughts or feelings that they often evoke:

	Positive	Negative
Red	bold, extroverted, powerful, energetic, sexy	angry, negative, warlike, lusty, competitive, impulsive, aggressive
Orange	friendly, outgoing, stimulating	gaudy, tacky, cheap
Yellow	warm, energetic, stimulating, cheerful	sickly, jaundiced, treacherous, deceitful
Green	financial, mature, soothing, holistic, growing, feisty, fresh, stable	sickly, spoiling, envious (green with envy), boring, frustrated
Blue	calming, soothing, spiritual, emotional, secure, trusting	depressed, passive, isolated, cold
Purple	majestic, spiritual, intuitive, genial, royal, scholarly	mournful, guilty, suffering, sad
Brown	steady, grounded, earthy, reliable, rich, physically comfortable or secure	boring, dull, greedy, stingy, muddy, awkward
White	clean, crisp, pure, whole	empty, bleak, blank, unemotional
Black	sophisticated, stately, formal, elegant, powerful	mournful, cruel, hostile, rebellious

3

Choosing Your Most Flattering Styles

No one wants to invest time and money in unflattering and ill-fitting clothing, which can be dreadful-looking. But somehow, through a combination of poor choices and insufficient knowledge about what is most flattering, that is exactly what can happen. There are guidelines that you can follow to make the most of your budget and wardrobe choices. Choosing well will help you to look great, feel great, and be well-dressed. Your best clothing selections will be based on a number of factors, such as your general bone structure, facial features and shape, height and weight, and how your body weight is distributed around your frame. Your personality, posture, age, and natural coloring must also be considered. Do not forget to factor in your lifestyle, environment, and economic conditions.

The line of the clothes you wear should be in harmony with the line of your body. If you have a very round body, do not choose very angular, severe fashions; aim for softer lines instead. The scale of your body and the scale of your clothes should also support each other. Do not wear huge, overpowering prints or patterns if you are very little or petite. Smaller patterns and prints are more suitable.

Let the texture and pattern of your fabrics harmonize with your lines. If you are very tall and angular, your choices will be different from someone who is short and heavy. If you are short-waisted with long legs, your approach to dressing will be different from that of someone who is long waisted with short legs. If you have full hips and narrow shoulders, your choices will be different than that of someone with wide shoulders and narrow hips. A rounded stomach presents its own kind of challenge.

Defining Your Clothing Personality

The clothes that you feel best in are usually the clothes that you look best in as well. You have a definite clothing personality; spend some time studying and evaluating what works best for you. A number of image consultants like to use the following clothing personality classifications: Dramatic, Natural, Classic, Romantic or Gamin. However, most people's clothing personalities will usually be a combination of two or more types. Remember to keep in mind what is appropriate to wear for a particular occasion. While you might love casual wear such as sweaters and jeans, they are not appropriate for business situations. Modify your look to suit the occasion. Today many items of clothing have become multifunctional; except for extremely dressy occasions, they can fit in anywhere with the right accessories.

The Gamin

The Gamin usually has a pleasant, animated, and expressive face. Energy and enthusiasm are projected. Body movements may be quick and well coordinated. The Gamin is usually small-boned and wiry, but strong. This is accompanied by a youthful look and outgoing mannerisms. Appearance is usually neat. Hairstyles and clothing are generally simple and uncomplicated.

The Romantic

Romantics project a certain softness (in women) or a suaveness (in men). Both have an understated sophistication. Romantics project charm and sex appeal and may even be flirty. Romantics may have very expressive eyes and features. They possess a magnetic personality and enjoy dressing with flair. Soft, curly hair styles, long or short, are often chosen by Romantic men and women.

The Classic

The Classic stays away from fads and leans towards simplicity and moderation in dress and mannerisms. A refined, traditional, and poised look is associated with the Classic. Classics may be reserved and may even appear formal and controlled. The Classic is usually well groomed with a simple, conservative hairstyle.

The Dramatic

The Dramatic will usually have interesting features and a lean body, whether tall or slight in build. The appearance is striking with an elegant, confident manner. The Dramatic projects worldliness and individuality. Unusual or high-fashion clothing is worn very well. For the women, severe, exotic hairstyles are often chosen.

<u>The Natural</u>

The Natural man or woman is usually relaxed and friendly, preferring a casual, comfortable, and informal approach to dressing. Naturals seem to gravitate to the outdoors and appear to be athletic, and they are generally well-toned with a wholesome look. Hairstyles are usually casual and relaxed.

Important Fashion Tips for Men

- Since your shirt and tie are closest to your face, always choose flattering colors and styles.
- Make sure that the color of your tie pulls your jacket and shirt together for a total look.
- Your shirt collar should not distract from your total look by being too tight or too loose.
- The collars of your shirt and jacket should be balanced in length and width.
- The cuffs of your shirt should be about a half inch below your jacket sleeve. Your wrist bone should not show.
- Your suit or jacket should not pull or pucker across the shoulders in back.
- If you are very tall, you should avoid horizontal lines in suits. Contrasting colors might work well for you.
- Avoid bold or horizontal patterns if you are very heavy.

- Vertical lines make one appear taller; use them to your advantage and avoid too much contrast in colors if you are shorter.
- Let the legs of your pants rest at your shoe heels with a break in the front.
- Keep shoes well polished.
- Avoid frayed or crinkled shirt collars and cuffs.
- Choose a suit or jacket in a neutral color for more versatility.
- Do not let your suit jacket pull across the front or at the buttons.
- Coordinate your socks with your shoes and pants for a harmonious look.

Let Your Suit Choice Match Your Body Build

- <u>Heavy or stocky:</u> Avoid a very tapered, tight fit. A more relaxed, loose style will be more flattering.
- <u>Slender:</u> A more defined or fitted shape can look very good on you and enhance the appeal of your figure.
- <u>Medium:</u> This allows for versatility. Choose what is most flattering.

Common Fashion Concerns of Women

- <u>Very tall:</u> Use contrasting colors and accessories, especially in belts. Wider belts are good. Horizontal lines and layering with heavier fabrics are good choices. Avoid clothes with high waists and short jackets that stop or break at the waist.
- <u>Very short:</u> Dressing in one color or variations of the same color works well. Avoid contrasting accessories (especially in belts), oversized, bulky clothing or accessories, and heavy layering. Vertical lines and

patterns work best for you. Use interesting details in the upper third of your body.

- Full-figured: Avoid horizontal lines and be careful of huge, busy prints or patterns and too much fullness, layering, or details. Vertical lines work best. Avoid tight fitting clothes. Draw attention to your face and wear attractive colors that flatter your face.
- Very thin: Use interesting patterns and layering. You can carry off details and fullness in your skirts and blouses. Bright colors work well for you. Use horizontal lines to your advantage, especially in belts. Wide panels, depending on your size, are also good for you.
- Wide waist: Choose styles that slim the body. Draw attention to your upper torso with details. Wear narrow belts in subtle colors, or colors that are the same as your outfit. Avoid horizontal lines at the waist area. A dropped waist is a good choice.
- Thin waist: Wide belts in bright, contrasting styles are great choices. Add interesting details at the waist area.
- Broad or squared shoulders: Avoid excessive use of shoulder pads or details and horizontal lines in the shoulder area. A raglan sleeve is very flattering. Choose a V-neck, but avoid halter tops. Add fullness in the skirt and wear brighter colors near the hip areas and pockets.
- Narrow shoulders: Set in sleeves or extended seams with epaulets or other details at the shoulder are flattering for you. However, avoid V-necks and raglan sleeves. Add shoulder pads, if desired. Wide lapels work well for you. Lighter colors in the torso areas and darker colors in your pants or skirts are desirable. Choose lapels that draw the eye

upward.

- Heavy arms: Avoid long, tight-fitting sleeves in shiny or clingy fabrics. Avoid sleeveless tops.
- Short waist: Use a narrow belt that is similar in color to your top instead of your skirt. A dropped waistline on your dress can be very appealing. Avoid pants and skirts with waistbands if possible.
- Long waist: Choose wide belts in contrasting colors or colors that match your skirt. Try to choose skirts, dresses, and pants with wide waistbands.
- Heavy thighs: Allow for fullness in your skirt or dress. At the waist, an A-line skirt can be very flattering. Avoid tapered pants. Draw attention to your upper torso with brighter colors and details.
- Heavy legs: Use darker tones of pantyhose and add some fullness in the skirt, especially around the hemline. Avoid shiny fabrics in your skirt. A-line styles are flattering and a good choice.
- Thin legs: Use lighter pantyhose and avoid too much fullness in the skirt area.
- Narrow hips: Focus details and attention around the waist area. Wear fuller skirts, pleats, and gathers for a flattering look. Hip pockets also add a flattering touch. Bright colors at the waist and in the skirt are good touches.
- Wide hips: Clothes that ease away from the waistline are good. Choose styles that skim the body such as vests and sweaters. Avoid tight skirts or extremely full skirts. Use darker colors in this area. Let the eye travel up to the details on the torso. Stay away from details such as pockets or

gathers at the hip line.

- Flat buttocks: Choose skirts or pants with fullness.
- Full buttocks: Choose soft lines that gradually ease away from the body such as an A-line skirt. Avoid skirts that are too straight.
- Full tummy: Use interesting details at the shoulders and the neckline. Avoid gathers or too many pleats at the waistline. A dropped waist and slashed pockets are flattering.
- Flat chest: Choose fullness in the upper garments. Don't show off too much cleavage. Add interesting details at the shoulders or in accessories.
- Full bust: Wear subtle colors on the upper portion of the body. Avoid accessories or too many details right at the bust-line as well as horizontal lines in that area. Items that show too much cleavage and items made of clingy fabrics are not good choices. Don't wear high-waisted clothing. Choose a narrow belt.

4

Stretching Your Fashion Dollar

There are many benefits to be derived from a wardrobe that's put together well. Armed with the proper attire, you should:

- look more attractive
- become more confident in coordinating your clothes
- feel good about yourself
- get more mileage out of the clothes you have instead of wearing only a small fraction of your wardrobe nearly all the time
- spend less money on clothes and make fewer mistakes when shopping
- have more options when dressing for a special occasion

Wardrobe Assessment

Before buying any new clothes or getting rid of any clothes, evaluate what you already have. Do not rush. Go through your closet and organize your clothes into three groups:

- clothes you always wear
- clothes you sometimes wear
- clothes you never wear

Analyze clothing according to color compatibility, style, design, texture, and patterns, as well how they fit you and how they go with your lifestyle. Your clothing should reflect your personality. First, take out the clothes that you consistently do not wear and pack them up for donation to a nonprofit organization. This might be hard to do, but you will feel good about giving them to a charitable group. Only keep them if you absolutely must. Next, the clothes that you only wear occasionally should be hung in the back of your closet. Use them until you are able to weed them out completely. Create a list of what you need.

Organizing Your Clothes

Now set up a system for organizing the remaining clothes. One of the secrets of putting together a great wardrobe is organization—this will give you a feeling of control over your wardrobe. You might want to organize your clothes by color or by similarity (all jackets together, all pants together, etc.). They can also be separated according to use. Do what makes you feel the most comfortable, and do the same for your accessories.

Once this is done, decide what you need to add to your wardrobe. Make a list based on your needs. From now on, buy only those things on the list that you need—in the right colors for you. They should be flattering, as well as practical for your lifestyle.

Now, it will be much easier to get dressed every day. You will begin to see wonderful, new clothing combinations at a glance. The clothing that you already have will give you more mileage and you will start to receive more compliments.

Other Clothing Needs

If you wear a uniform at work, make sure that it is always fresh, neat and free of stains. If you wear casual clothes to work before changing into your uniform, the same rule applies. Assume that someone is observing you at all times. Your appearance both in and out of uniform may be a factor when promotions are considered.

Building a Basic Wardrobe

In building a wardrobe, there are some basic pieces that you will need. Depending on your lifestyle, you might need more of some pieces and fewer of other items. If you seldom need business attire, this should be reflected in your wardrobe. Study what you have and see where you need to fill in for a well-coordinated and functional wardrobe. Subtract or add in each category according to your lifestyle.

You may want to follow versions of basic wardrobes as suggested by

Carole Jackson in *Color Me Beautiful* and *Color For Men.*

Basic Wardrobe for Women

Your clothing needs will vary according to your lifestyle. All clothing should be in your most flattering neutral or basic colors. Choose the best quality that you can afford.

- Jacket: The starting point for any basic wardrobe is a good, versatile jacket (either suit or blazer style). Watch for a good sale or try a local reputable thrift store, if necessary—they have many wonderful quality items at a fraction of the original cost. Quality clothing will last longer, even with a lot of wear and cleaning. They also retain their shape better.
- Skirt: If possible, choose a skirt in the same fabric and color as the jacket. Then you can create the look of a suit. You can choose a contrasting color or subtle pattern as long as it is neutral or basic and works well with your jacket.
- Suit: Choose a classic style in the best fabric that you can afford.
- Pants: A solid color will be more versatile than a patterned pair. You can wear a dressy blouse with them and create an attractive evening look. A neutral or basic color will go with a variety of blouses or skirts.
- Dress (1 or 2): Your first dress should be simple and versatile in style. Let your accessories take your dress in the direction that you choose—dressier or more casual. There are wonderful two-piece dresses suitable for mixing and matching to stretch your fashion budget. The top makes

a wonderful blouse for a suit. The skirt, combined with another blouse, creates a dressy or casual outfit.

- Blouses (3): Choose a tailored blouse that is simple enough to work well with a business suit and elegant enough to create a dressy look. The second blouse should be casual enough to wear with pants or skirts but not limited to casual wear. The third blouse can have a dressy feel to it, but still offer flexibility for less dressy occasions. A basic, versatile pattern is a good choice in one of your blouses.
- Sweater: Choose your sweater in a style that can be dressed up with the right blouse and jewelry. Let it provide a more relaxed touch when desired by using the right accessories.
- Coat: Consider a style that is simple and practical; it should not fade in popularity in a season or two. Buy the best quality that you can afford, especially in such an important item. An additional coat only for dressy occasions is not practical unless you attend a lot of social affairs and your budget permits the purchase.
- Casual clothes: Fill in as you need them, as your budget permits and as your lifestyle dictates. These are great for designated dress down days at work, especially for casual Fridays. However, even when you dress down remember to be conscious of your appearance—do not go to the extreme.

Basic Wardrobe for Men

- Suit: Choose a suit that fits you well. Select a darker neutral shade that can be used for dressy occasions, for work, or more casual occasions.

Depending on where in the country you live, the fabric can be heavy or light. Region and climate will also affect the color you choose. Lighter colors and fabrics are usually worn in warmer climates, and darker colors and heavier fabrics are usually preferred in colder, rainy climates. A suit with a vest gives added versatility.

- Sport jacket: This is suitable for times when you want to make a good impression without appearing too formal. You will get more wear out of a solid neutral color, which will be more practical than a patterned jacket. A sport jacket will also be very comfortable when traveling and will still look attractive.
- Dress pants (2): Your pants should be of good quality in colors that work well with your sport coat, sweater, and shirt. If you choose not to wear a jacket or sweater, your pants should still look good with your shirt. They should also offer versatility and comfort. Choose a basic style.
- Shirts (3): One of these shirts should be in a neutral white or cream color and suitable for a dressy event. Choose the color that is most flattering for you. The size and style of the collar should also flatter your face. One of the shirts can be casual and have a pattern as long as it blends well with your pants and sport jacket. Let one shirt be broad-based and versatile enough for dressing up or down.
- Ties (3): Choose one tie in a solid color that will go with everything in your wardrobe. It should be in a color that is flattering to you since it is near your face. Let it work well with all of your shirts, including a patterned one. One of the other ties can have a pattern, but it should always pull together your suit or jacket with your shirt. A tie in a striped

pattern is also a good choice if you like the look. This will offer you more variety.

- Casual pants: Today's casual pants can be attractive, practical, and comfortable with a sport jacket, a shirt and tie, or with a sweater for lounging. Aim for comfort and neutral colors.
- Casual shirt: You should feel comfortable and relaxed in it. You may want to consider an additional casual shirt in a pattern for more variety.
- Sweater: A simple style or a basic color will give you a lot of wear. It can be worn with casual or dress slacks.
- Overcoat: An all-purpose coat with a warm zip-in lining can be very practical and can replace a regular coat. It can be casual or dressy. Depending on your lifestyle, a shorter-length jacket may be sufficient for your needs.
- Casual clothes: Add as you need them, as your budget permits and as your lifestyle dictates. These are especially good when permitted in the work place on designated casual attire days, like casual Fridays.

As you extend your basic wardrobe, you can add pieces with patterns which will help to give you more variety. Choose colors, styles, details, fabrics, lines, and textures that work well with each other. You probably have some of these items in your wardrobe. Look at what you already own and work around these pieces.

Note: Select your neutrals and basics in coordinated colors so that they are able to harmonize with each other.

What To Do About Your Wardrobe Mistakes

Few people can afford to go out and buy an entire wardrobe at once. You can, however, slowly weed out those clothes that have proven to be less-than-perfect choices. For now, you can mix them with items that look really well on you. If you have a suit that is not in a good color for you, add a blouse or shirt in a flattering color. Mix your less attractive clothes with accessories that are flattering to you in color and style.

Choose Clothes that Are Practical for Your Lifestyle

Your clothing needs will be different if you are a student, a housewife, a business person, or a carpenter. When planning your wardrobe, think about your hobbies and social life. If you travel a great deal, take this into consideration: There are many wonderful wrinkle-resistant fabrics that travel well and still look fresh when you arrive at your destination. Before buying anything new, evaluate what you already have on hand to see if it serves your current needs. You will also need to estimate how much time you spend on various activities. The activity you spend the most time on should be reflected proportionately in your clothing budget. If it is not, rearrange your budget.

Shopping

When you do find it necessary to shop, there are a few basic rules that you should follow. Use discipline—buy what you really need first. If you need to make major changes, buy your basics first.

- Never, but *never* go shopping when you are feeling fatigued. Your judgment will be less accurate when deciding what best suits your needs. For this reason, it is best to shop early in the day, when you are rested and thinking clearly. Wear comfortable shoes and clothing that are easy to remove when trying on garments.
- Try to avoid shopping on deadline for a special occasion. You might choose something that you will not like later on, and you will not get much wear out of it.
- Be thoroughly familiar with what you already have in your closet. This will help you to know if your new purchase will add mileage to what you already own. If necessary, take color samples with you so that you do not buy the wrong colors.
- Buy fewer clothing items of better quality. They will fit better, look better, and last longer, and they will not lose their shape in one or two seasons.
- When trying on clothes, do not guess about sizes, which vary according to each manufacturer. Even if you are tired and feel sure that the item you are purchasing will fit you, it is still better to try it on. If it does not fit, you will have saved the time and energy you would have spent returning it later. Also, something might look wonderful on the rack, but you might not like it when you actually try it on.
- Be careful when shopping with friends or co-workers. Colors and styles reflect personal preferences; a particular style or color might look terrific on someone else but be completely wrong for you. Be careful of the opinions of salespeople as well.

- Avoid impulsive shopping. Do not buy something just because it is a great buy or on sale. If it is not the right color or style for you, chances are it will hang in your closet after one or two wearings. It then becomes a very expensive item. Do not buy something just because you are having a bad day or feeling depressed—it might not be something you will want later.

Take Care of Your Clothing

Your clothing should be ready to wear at all times. Ripped seams and missing buttons make a garment useless for the moment. Take care of repairs immediately—otherwise, you might forget to do it. Keep shoes repaired and shined. The item you need for that unexpected occasion might be the very item that is not available.

Have clothing cleaned as needed so that your clothes will be fresh at all times. Once body odor and perspiration settle in to clothing, especially manmade fabrics, they are very hard to remove—some clothes are even ruined. Good-quality, natural-fiber clothing will hold up better under constant wear and cleaning because the fabric and construction are usually better.

Hang your clothes as soon as you take them off. Use the proper hangers for skirts, pants, and jackets. Padded hangers are good for delicate or soft fabrics. Remove all items from your pockets.

Travel

Your destination, your mode of travel, how long you will stay, and the reason for your trip will all influence what you will pack. Pack as lightly as possible but take sufficient clothing. If you are traveling by plane, you will want to dress comfortably but also look stylish. You may want to be more casual and comfortable if you are traveling by car or train. In any case, try to choose fabrics that are wrinkle-resistant and easy to wash and dry overnight.

Take clothes that can be mixed and matched to create different outfits, unless you need a business suit, obviously. Use a couple of neutral or basic colors, and add variety with your accessories. Pick up colors in your scarves or blouses. Choose accessories, especially shoes, handbags, and ties, that work with the clothing that you are taking. Jewelry should be versatile and practical. Make sure that you have comfortable shoes, because your feet often swell during travel and this will be aggravated by ill-fitting shoes. Traveling with several overloaded suitcases should be a thing of the past.

Fads

Fads come and go quickly and there will always be new styles and colors in fashion. Some are quite appealing and you might look wonderful in them. However, do not choose an expensive suit or coat in a very trendy color or style; while you might get many wonderful compliments now, this item could be out of style in the next season or two.

Try adding trendy colors or styles in inexpensive accessories such as a tie, shirt or blouse, scarves, or inexpensive jewelry. They can update your wardrobe and create that trendy look without requiring a lot of money.

Accessorizing

Your accessories can give your true personality a chance to shine through, whether you are dressing for work or for a casual event. Your accessories should be in harmony with the line and scale of your clothing and with your best colors, lifestyle, facial features, size, body proportions, and personality. Accessories can boost your wardrobe by coordinating, enhancing, and personalizing what you already own. Accessories consist of hosiery, socks, hats, suspenders, handkerchiefs, shoes, gloves, glasses, goggles, handbags, briefcases, scarves, belts, jewelry, bows, boots, and more. Your most important accessories should always be of a good quality, in neutral colors, and in basic styles.

When you are accessorizing, choose one main focal point of interest. Too many details can be distracting and make your clothes look inexpensive or gaudy.

<u>For women, some of your most important accessories are as follows:</u>

- <u>Shoes:</u> Better-quality shoes will last and keep their shape longer. A basic shoe in quality leather is a good choice. The color should be neutral and match your clothing. A basic pump or slip-on shoe is very versatile. For a trip, pack one or two pairs of shoes in neutral colors to go with everything that you will wear. Always pack a pair of casual shoes. Keep shoes polished and avoid scuff marks.
- <u>Scarves:</u> Scarves can give the same basic outfit many different looks. They should be in the right proportion to your size and in the right colors. Scarves are a great neutralizer because they can place your most flattering colors close to your face and help to balance an otherwise unflattering outfit. When traveling, they can multiply the number of looks you can create from a few basic pieces. Often, people have many

lovely scarves, tucked away in drawers going to waste.

- Hats: Make sure that they match your size, match your personality, and face shape. Hats are no longer a must; they are optional unless you live in a cold climate.
- Glasses: Your features, face shape and size, general coloring, and hairstyle all should influence your glasses—their shape, their size, and their color. Your lifestyle and personality must also be considered. If you choose a metal frame, choose it in a flattering color.
- Belts: Belts can add variety to your wardrobe, and a good quality belt can enhance your outfit. A belt in a contrasting color can appear to reduce your height. If you are petite or short-waisted, a thinner belt is a good choice. If you are very tall, you might want to try a wide belt in a contrasting color.
- Gloves: Gloves come and go in fashion unless you live in a cold climate. Gloves can be worn in neutral colors, or in deeper colors as accent pieces.
- Jewelry: The right jewelry personalizes and enhances an outfit. Your jewelry should be in balance and harmony with your face size and shape, neck length, lifestyle, and personality. It should be in the right color and size for you. If you wear cool colors best, choose white or softer-colored metals, and if you are drawn to gold jewelry, choose a white gold. If instead you look better in warm colors, choose richer, darker metals, especially in gold jewelry. Your jewelry can create different looks for you and give you a lot of versatility. Earrings should be chosen first.
- Hosiery: Neutral colors are more practical. Contrasting colors can chop

your clothing line. A color similar to the color of your skirt, dress, or pants can give you a long, leaner, symmetrical and unbroken line.

- Handbags: Do not let your handbag overpower your overall appearance. Pick one in a basic style and the right proportion for you. It should be in a neutral color that goes with your shoes. Handbags should be simple and of good quality. Many women prefer a shoulder bag for everyday wear. Handbags are used in all shapes, sizes, and colors today as accessories, but go with a basic one first.
- Briefcase: Quality in a briefcase is a must. Choose the best quality that you can afford. Choose the right proportion and size for you. A neutral color is the most practical.

5

Looking Fit and Fabulous

Exercise and Diet

Once you have picked out your best colors and invested in your wardrobe, having an attractive body will complement those choices. Exercise and proper nutrition add to your personal appeal, and your diet and exercise routine will help you attain great skin and hair. Most people want a body that looks fit and well-toned and it is only natural to want to be energetic and active. Avoiding a sedentary lifestyle is important, and planning, exercise, and a proper diet are a must.

Major Benefits of Exercising

- Your body burns fat faster.
- Your circulation improves.
- You have lower levels of fatigue and stress.
- You fight off the effects of aging.
- You sleep better at night.
- You have an improved general sense of balance.
- You have greater endurance.
- You look better.
- Your skin gets cleaner and clearer.
- Your heart strengthens.
- You become more mentally alert.

Getting Started

The longer you put off exercising, the harder it will be to get started and the harder you'll have to work to strengthen your muscles. The key is to find the right exercise program and to stick with it. Exercise must be an essential and routine part of your life in order for it to be effective. Check with your doctor before beginning any workout program. Exercise need not be painful or exhausting—try to focus on some aspect of it that you enjoy doing. For example, stretching for a few minutes upon rising each morning is an excellent way to start the day. You can squeeze workout opportunities into your daily routine or schedule, such as climbing stairs rather than using an elevator or walking to the store instead of driving, when possible.

When you find a form of exercise that you enjoy, you will be less prone to procrastinate. It is better to have some form of exercise daily, even for a few minutes, rather than intense but sporadic workouts, which can also be dangerous. It is necessary to make a regular daily habit of exercising so that it becomes part of your daily schedule and lifestyle. Dress comfortably for exercise, wear the proper footwear for support, and breathe freely and regularly.

Forms of Exercising

There are simple, wonderful, and enjoyable forms of exercise for almost everyone. Whatever you do, start slowly in the beginning. One of the best, most uncomplicated forms of exercise is walking. It is a wonderful exercise for beginners, is terrific for maintaining your weight, and is very enjoyable. Walking does not require a lot of planing or expensive equipment. It is uncomplicated and allows flexibility in your schedule. You can start walking at a slow pace and increase your pace later. You can also accomplish little chores along the way such as buying a newspaper, dropping off dry cleaning, or simply enjoying nature. Swimming is another enjoyable form of exercise, and it is also refreshing. Many people enjoy dancing in one form or another, and it rarely seems like exercise. Choose the form of dancing that is most enjoyable to you—the music alone will help to motivate you. Avoid strenuous forms of dancing if you are not in good shape. Other good choices include tennis, golf, bicycle riding, and canoeing.

If you are overweight or have not been exercising on a regular basis, *start slowly*. Remember, consult a physician about the proper program for you. Do not let anyone talk you into doing exercises that you are not prepared for or able to do—you are the best judge of what is happening in your body and what you are feeling. Always take time to stretch and warm up prior to exercising. Also, allow yourself time to stretch again after exercising, in order to cool down.

Exercise Mistakes to Avoid

- not warming up before exercising or cooling down afterwards
- failing to use the correct techniques
- working out on the wrong surface
- not resting when your body tells you to do so
- exercising until you are in pain

Nutrition

How you eat also directly affects how you look and feel. A poor diet cannot be helped with makeup, a full beard or oversized clothing. Skin that appears dull and dry, is oily, or is marked with blackheads or whiteheads, may be the result of a poor diet. If skin appears rosy, vibrant, and alive, proper eating habits may have played a role in this as well.

Additionally, your diet is as related to your emotional state as it is to your physical state. Food plays a very important part in life today. One of the most popular pastimes is eating, and more and more, people are turning to comfort food. Many people associate food with love and warmth, caring, and enjoyment. You are constantly bombarded with tantalizing food advertisements on television commercials and on billboards. Some restaurants are beautiful and enticing and promise relaxation—dining in an enjoyable atmosphere. Others are intimate and romantic—just what would be appealing to lovers. Convenient fast-food restaurants greet you on every corner and make it convenient for you to appease your appetite immediately. And do not forget constant coffee or snack breaks. It is no wonder that you are constantly bombarded with temptation.

In spite of all of this, it is necessary to educate and re-educate yourself about what you are putting into your body. Get to know the nutritional value of what you are eating and how your diet affects you. Food choices for some people are directly affected by what is stylish. You have been told, for example, that you can never be too thin, and in an attempt to bend to fashion, you can damage your body by denying yourself the right nutritional foods that are needed for good health. It is hard to decide what to eliminate from your diet in order to achieve a balance between your figure and your health. Fad diets are constantly being promoted as the ultimate, overnight success, but they are often unhealthy and can be dangerous. Any extreme diet should be avoided.

On the other hand, many people are overweight. Before starting any kind of dieting program, consult a doctor because obesity may be the result of a number of causes. Losing weight too quickly can cause wrinkling and loss of muscle tone. It can also be dangerous. Losing weight is something that should be done slowly and consistently. Do not eliminate important nutrients from your diet while losing weight. Once the desired goal is achieved, follow a realistic maintenance program, and do not forget that each person's dietary situation is different.

You can also control *when* and *how* you eat. It will help you to lose weight if you chew food more slowly and thoroughly. The meal will be more filling as well. You will digest your food better and feel less hungry. Smaller meals eaten more frequently are also better than huge, unevenly spaced meals. <u>Consider the following in dieting:</u>

- When a diet is too strenuous, it is harder to maintain.
- It is important to re-educate yourself about the danger of any excessive eating patterns.
- The more weight that you have gained, the more difficult it will be to lose.

Tips on Good Eating

- Do not wait until you are famished to eat.
- Never grocery shop when you are hungry.
- Eat fresh fruit or drink fresh fruit juice for a natural source of sugar.
- Eliminate—or at least limit—your intake of refined flours and sugars.
- Eat fewer fatty foods, especially fried products.
- Avoid excessive snacking.
- Cut down on salt and unsaturated fats.
- Drink lots of water.
- Avoid processed foods.

What you eat can have a definite effect on your mood and temperament. There are many foods that rob the body of nutrition and make you nervous and irritable, while other foods nourish and calm the body. Too much coffee or tea can deplete you of energy and cause sugar levels to drop, making you nervous and resulting in a need for more food. A cup of coffee and a doughnut or pastry is not a good way to start the day. It is not good preparation for an important appointment, job interview, or sales presentation, because it will definitely not give you the "thinking power" you need.

Avoid the following:

- weight loss programs that are too strenuous and unrealistic
- fasting or starving yourself, which can be very dangerous to your health
- rapid weight losses and gains, which can cause loss of muscle tone and sagging
- unhealthy binging and starvation, which can cause bloating, especially in the face

Nutritional Necessities

Find out all you can about the kinds of foods that you are eating. What nutritional value do they have? Are they nothing but empty calories? Assess your diet to see if you are getting the vitamins, minerals, proteins, carbohydrates, and healthy fats that you need. All of these nutrients play a vital role in keeping you healthy and attractive. Try to add more fresh fruits and vegetables to your diet, as well as whole grains. Fresh fruits are an excellent way to satisfy a sweet tooth or sugar craving and are much healthier. Vegetables also have a much greater nutritional value when not overcooked.

Water, Water—Never Enough

The importance of drinking enough water cannot be stressed enough. Water is something that you take for granted, yet you cannot live without it. Without sufficient water, you become dehydrated, as well as fatigued because your body is from one half to two-thirds water. Water also has a tremendous effect on the skin and complexion: It prevents fatty deposits of oil from settling on the surface and creating blackheads and whiteheads. At least eight 8-ounce glasses of water daily are *usually* needed by the body in order to detoxify it and keep it balanced, but this may vary with each person.

<u>Water also provides the following additional benefits:</u>

- It helps the body burn stored fats.
- It decreases one's appetite.
- It helps to moisturize the skin.
- It acts as a hydrator, smoothing and softening the texture of the skin.
- It aids in digestion.
- It facilitates the necessary removal of body waste.

6

Skin and Body Care

It's a Treat, Not a Chore

Healthy and attractive skin enhances your personal appeal enormously. It is a reflection of the commitment you make to yourself—how you take care of yourself in general, as well as how much time and attention you devote to your skin. Taking good care of your skin should always be an important goal. Proper nutrition, sufficient rest and sleep, exercise, and lots of water are vital to your skin. Proper cleansing, moisturizing, and protection are also essential, and you will reap the benefits for the rest of your life.

The look and feel of your skin is determined by external and internal factors:

- general daily habits, including diet
- natural elements—the sun, dryness, humidity, cold, heat, general pollution
- amount of relaxation and sleep
- air conditioning
- genetics
- stress
- water
- age
- exercise
- alcohol and tobacco
- illness
- lifestyle

Your skin performs a number of vital functions. It regulates body temperature and acts as a thermostat. It also rids the body of waste materials through perspiration, while retaining vital fluids within the body. The skin keeps out pollutants and screens out ultraviolet rays. It also plays a major role in your appearance, as well as shaping your body and face.

Composition of Skin

The skin is the outer shell and cover of the body and it is in a constant state of flux and change. Your skin consists of two primary layers—the epidermis and the dermis. The epidermis is the layer of the skin that you actually see. It is your protective layer and is fed cells on an ongoing basis from the dermis. Keratin, a protein-based substance, is found in the epidermis. As these cells move upward, they are flattened and overlap in layers to provide a protective covering for the skin. Cells in the epidermis are continually being shed.

The dermis is beneath the epidermis and contains living cells, sweat glands, blood vessels, fatty tissue, nerve endings, and sebaceous glands. Sebum, an oil substance, is produced by the sebaceous glands, hair follicles and the amount of sebum produced determines the condition of your skin as well as your skin type. As you can see, proper nourishment is important to ensure the proper functioning of the dermis. Collagen, the protein that affects your skin's elasticity, is found here.

Basic Skin Types

There are five basic skin types. Try to recognize yours and care for it accordingly.

<u>Dry skin</u>

- may feel dry to the touch
- may look palc and dry
- is prone to chapping and flaking
- develops wrinkles and lines easily
- lacks an adequate moisture and oil balance

<u>Normal skin</u>

- is supple and clear

- has an even distribution of oil and moisture
- has a smooth appearance

Oily skin

- is oily when touched
- can have enlarged pores
- is prone to skin eruptions
- can appear greasy
- has excessive oil

Combination skin

- has an oily T-zone (forehead, chin and nose area)
- has drier temple, eye, cheeks, and throat areas

Sensitive skin

- is often blotchy and uneven
- can appear translucent
- responds quickly to environmental changes
- is susceptible to allergic reactions

Skin Care

You should follow a skin care program that is good for your skin type. It should be followed in the morning and evening for best results. Try to be consistent. A good skin care program should consist of the following:

Cleansing agents (or cleansers)

Cleanliness is necessary for healthy skin. Proper cleansing allows your pores to breathe more fully. A cleanser removes all dead skin cells, dirt, makeup, and excess oil. Cleansers come in a variety of forms: soaps, creams, facial washes, and lotions. If you have dry skin, avoid soap because some soaps can be very drying. Some cleansers are formulated to eliminate the use of toners or astringents.

Toners or astringents

Toners and astringents perform a double function. The right toner should restore your skin's acid balance. They remove any lingering traces of dirt or cleansers and close the pores for protection from the environment. Toners usually contain no alcohol and are better for dry skin. Astringents are more suitable for oily skin because they usually contain varying degrees of alcohol, which helps with eliminating any trace of oils. Use after you cleanse and before your moisturizer. Avoid the eye area.

Moisturizers

Moisturizers assist the skin in maintaining moisture, which helps the skin to stay balanced in water content and stay soft. This helps to minimize fine lines and wrinkles. They also serve as protection from natural elements and the environment and help to ward off wrinkles. They can be used alone or under makeup. Choose one with a sunscreen.

Exfoliation

This is a process that supports your regular cleansing routine. It uproots any embedded dirt or excess oil and allows the cells underneath to breathe more. There are many natural products on the market today that make great exfoliants. One of the most popular is a honey and almond scrub. Avoid exfoliating in the eye area. Avoid harsher products that can damage your skin. Use gently.

Masks

Masks can be soothing and give your skin an attractive and smooth appearance. There are masks in different strengths and for different purposes. The most popular ones are for deep cleansing, stimulating, toning, tightening and moisturizing—depending on your skin type. They are generally used once or twice a week. Avoid the eye area when applying a mask.

Hand And Nail Care

The hands and nails are usually the most neglected parts of your body, yet they need special attention and care—as much as the rest of your body. The hands and nails can reveal a person's hobbies, work, interests, lifestyle, age, and degree of care.

Diet is also very important to your hands and nails. Stubby, broken nails are often the result of missing essential nutrients in the diet. When attending a special event, giving a presentation, or interviewing for a job, pay special attention to your hands. Well-maintained hands show how much you care about yourself. This helps to make a positive impression. Some important tips for the care of the hands and nails:

- Moisturize frequently.
- Pay attention to your diet.
- Use rubber gloves for household cleaning.
- Wear heavy gloves for harsh activities or when gardening.
- Do not use your nails to open jars or other containers.
- Wear gloves in cold weather.
- Pay attention to a chipped or broken nail right away.
- Try to schedule a manicure at home or in a salon on a regular basis.

Exposure to the Sun

While the sun performs many wonderful functions, it can be very harmful to your skin. Skin cancer—as well as premature aging—can be caused by too much sun. Everyone should be aware of ultraviolet radiation from the sun's rays.

Good sunscreen is essential for both men and women to maintain healthy skin. This will block most of the sun's damaging ultraviolet rays. All skin needs protection regardless of type. When you are exposed to the sun, be sure to do the following:

- Make sure that your skin is protected at all times.
- Wear sunscreen outdoors even when in mild, cloudy, or hazy weather.
- Use a sunscreen on all exposed areas of your body.
- Use of an SPF-rated (Sun Protection Factor) sunscreen should be used even if you are swimming because ultraviolet rays can penetrate water. Also remember to apply it after you get out of the water.

Body Care

Good body care always starts with staying clean. It is impossible to cover up offensive or stale body odor. Good body cleansing also has a very positive effect on how you feel because bathing is at the core of good grooming. You feel fresh and at ease in the presence of other people.

Cleanse your skin without handling it too harshly—the goal is to have clear and supple skin. Also, use gentle soaps or body cleansers that do not strip your body of vital oils. Always remember to moisturize your body as well as your face and hands. Natural oils from your body are lost on a regular basis, and this can cause dryness—but be careful to use a moisturizer that is not too oily, which can stain your clothing. It is best to moisturize your body when it is slightly damp. Whenever you bathe, rinse well to prevent your skin from drying out from soap cleanser residue. Also, avoid the continual use of excessive hot water, which will dry out your skin.

Foot Care

When your feet do not feel good, you do not feel good; good care of your feet is as important as the care of any other part of your body. Keep toenails neatly trimmed. Find time to soak your feet occasionally to prevent calluses, and moisturize them on a regular basis. A pedicure is a wonderful treat for your feet, whether done at home or professionally. Fresh socks or panty hose are always a treat for your feet as well. If you find odors building up in your shoes, pick up one of the many products on the market that can eliminate this problem. Many people have had a bad experience when someone else was not so considerate.

Tips for Pampering Your Feet

- Always buy shoes that fit in both length and width to avoid bunions, calluses, and corns, which can be very painful and hard to remove. They might even require costly and time-consuming professional care.
- Try shoes on in the store. If shoes do not fit in the store, they probably will not fit any better at home.
- If (for some reason) you have to wear ill-shaped or stiffly-styled shoes, do not wear them any longer than necessary.
- Your feet should be dried well after cleaning them.

Skin Eruptions

Be careful when handling pimples and breakouts in order to avoid infections or leaving a scar. Make sure your hands are clean before touching your face or handling your skin. Watch out for allergic reactions to certain products, food items, and skin-care products. Stress, medications, and hormonal changes can also be responsible for skin conditions. If this is a recurring problem for you, be especially careful to keep your skin clean, so that a build-up of dead skin cells, excessive dirt, oil, and bacteria does not block the pores. It might become necessary to schedule an appointment with a dermatologist for skin eruptions or any other recurring skin disorder, especially if they make you self-conscious and overly sensitive about how you look.

Deodorant

After a thorough body-cleansing in the bath or shower, it is usually necessary for most people to use deodorant for protection from body odor—particularly if you plan to be in the presence of other people.

Some people are concerned about chemicals in deodorants; in this case, you can find a product made out of natural ingredients. It is difficult to concentrate on someone's charms while planning to escape from that person's presence because of unpleasant body odor.

Teeth

Proper care of teeth is a must because a beautiful smile is a stunning asset. It is still good advice to brush your teeth twice a day and even after each meal, if possible. Schedule regular visits with your dentist just as you would with your doctor. Make flossing a regular part of your self-care routine. An attractive smile goes hand-in-hand with attractive teeth. Try to avoid tobacco stains on your teeth from cigarettes; coffee and tea can also leave unattractive stains with cotinual use.

You are never too old to have braces if you need them. The old stigma attached to wearing braces has been replaced by practicality, and corrective and cosmetic dentistry has become very sophisticated. If you have to have teeth removed, try to replace them with permanent bridgework or implants if possible; this will help to retain the shape of your mouth. Discolored teeth can be whitened with modern technology. Once again, get all the necessary information on the procedure that you are interested in before making a decision.

Red, Bleary Eyes

Bloodshot eyes can mar an otherwise attractive appearance. It gives an impression of illness, tiredness, or too many late nights. It sends a message that you are not quite up to the occasion at hand or that your energy level is low (in addition to making you look physically unattractive). To soothe your eyes, try using cold compresses to bathe your eyes in cool water. Eye drops are sometimes used to relieve red, irritated eyes, but it is best to consult a doctor, especially if bloodshot eyes are a persistent problem.

Smoking

In addition to the health problems caused by smoking, smokers are often unaware of how the smell of cigarette smoke penetrates clothing, hair, hands, and nails and how it lingers on the breath. Many nonsmokers find this offensive. If you smoke, be sensitive to others and think about when it is appropriate to smoke and when it might be offensive. If you are in a situation that is not appropriate for smoking (or where smoking is not allowed), you may want to excuse yourself and step outside. During a job interview, definitely refrain from smoking.

Chapped Lips

Chapped lips can mar an otherwise attractive appearance. However, there are many wonderful products on the market today for chapped lips. They protect and nourish the lips while enhancing your appearance. Some products usually are rich in vitamin E, which is nourishing and protective. Today many lipsticks and lip glosses provide sun and wind protection for your lips.

Fresh Breath

If you know that you have an important meeting, sales presentation, job interview, or a special date—or any social occasion—take extra care with your breath. Bad breath can result from any number of causes. It might be due to health problems, diet, poor hygiene, or smoking. Use mouthwash in addition to flossing and brushing for fresh, clean breath.

Fragrances

Fragrances can make you feel good about yourself. They should reflect your identity, your mood and your personality. Your fragrances should be as carefully selected as your other accessories; they should identify you, but always in a subtle way. It is the mark of your individuality. Adding your favorite fragrance after cleansing your body of stale body odor and perspiration is something wonderful for your body—it should be the finishing touch to your grooming procedure.

Your fragrance can have as much effect on you as it does on other people. Experiment to find the fragrance that is right for you. Keep your daytime fragrances particularly subtle; since the choice of fragrance is so personal, people in a business environment might not appreciate your fragrance, and there is less chance of offending if the scent is subtle. You can add more fragrance for the evenings when you are in a more personal situation.

Each person will experience different reactions to fragrances due to personal body chemistry. Be aware of the following when choosing and wearing a fragrance:

- Fragrances should never be too strong or overpowering.
- They should be subtle and in harmony with your personality.
- Fragrances come in different strengths.
- Do not buy the same fragrance as your friend without testing it on yourself first—it might not suit you.
- You might want to use different fragrances for different occasions.

7

Caring for Your Crowning Glory

It is most people's dream to have a head of healthy, beautiful, shiny hair that's styled perfectly. In order to help achieve this goal, proper hair care is essential. Knowing the background and basic characteristics of your hair will help you create your own hair-care system.

Your hair helps to insulate your body; it protects you from too much heat and holds on to body heat when necessary. Your hair is also continually growing, resting, shedding, and replacing itself. However, all of your hair is not undergoing the same cycle at the same time. Your hair grows at an average rate of a half inch per month, and the average person has from 100,000 to 150,000 individual hairs.

Each hair consists of a shaft, which lies above the surface of the skin, and a root, which is below the skin in a pitted area known as a follicle. The shaft consists of three layers: the cuticle, an outer layer containing overlapping cells; the cortex, which contains the pigment responsible for your hair color; and the medulla, which contains a looser, spongy array of cells. The follicle has what's called a sebaceous gland connected to it, and this produces sebum, a substance oily in nature and responsible for helping the hair stay lubricated and soft.

Hairstyle

Your hairstyle should draw attention to your face in a flattering way. A good haircut is the basis of any good style. It should highlight your best features. Your hair should be trimmed every six to eight weeks. See Chapter 8 for suggested hairstyles based on the shape of your face.

Your hairstyle is another beauty tool, so use it wisely; remember that how it looks will affect other people's impressions of you. Your hairstyle can make you appear unapproachable if it is too severe, or it can flatter you and improve your appearance. Do not scrimp in this area; a good style is a very wise investment. Just like any other accessory, your hairstyle should always suit the occasion.

There are some important factors to consider when choosing a hairstyle:

- type and texture of hair (thin or thick, limp or bouncy, curly or straight, wavy or kinky, long or short)

- personality
- face shape
- lifestyle
- body proportion and size
- time available for hair care
- age
- chemical treatments (relaxed or permed)

Be wary of trying a new hairstyle just because it is trendy; do not let a stylist talk you into trying something if you do not want it. Also, your best friend's hairstyle might be totally unsuitable or unflattering on you. But you should avoid the pattern of wearing the same hairstyle that you have always worn just because you are used to it—this can give you a very dated appearance. If you want to try something more modern, you can try a similar or updated shape of the same style instead of making a radical change.

Your lifestyle plays a major role in the kind of hairstyle you choose. If you are constantly on the go and have little time to devote to setting, blow drying and styling your hair, then a simple, shorter hairstyle is probably best for you. If you are athletic or spend a lot of time exercising and must constantly wash and condition your hair, shorter hair will work better for you as well.

Also, the type of hair you have will affect your hairstyle. Thin hair tends to appear limp if not cut well; it can appear fuller with the right hair cut. Thick hair can be easier to care for if it is layered.

Make sure that you communicate clearly with your stylist. Make sure he or she understands exactly what you want. Tell your stylist about yourself and what your needs are. Never assume that your stylist knows exactly what you want—Speak up! This puts your stylist in a better position to give you what you want and give you a style that is both flattering and practical. Do not be afraid to ask someone with similar hair texture and a hairstyle that you admire for the name of his or her stylist or barber. Most people respond well to this compliment and will be more than happy to do so. If there is something that you do not like about your haircut or style, discuss it before leaving the salon. Often it can be taken care of immediately. Ask for tips in maintaining your style—even the best style will not benefit you if you cannot duplicate it at home.

Typical Hair Conditions

- Dry hair has a dull, lifeless appearance and is harsh or brittle to the touch. The ends are usually damaged and split, and breakage occurs easily. The shaft of your hair is not being properly lubricated due to inadequate moisture and oil in the right balance. Avoid excessive heat. Use a good moisturizing conditioner and a gentle shampoo. Hot oil treatments can also help dry hair.
- Oily hair usually has no body because it is greasy and heavy. Oil builds up too quickly from the sebaceous glands. It often looks dirty, and it's very difficult to get oily hair to hold a style.
- Normal hair is the most desired hair type because it is not too dry or too oily. It has the right balance of moisture and oil. Be thankful.
- Dandruff is a condition that can mar an otherwise perfect appearance. It is usually very noticeable. It can be caused by a number of factors—

there is no one reason. However, the end results are excessive flaking of dead skin cells that fall noticeably on your shoulders, often visible at the most inappropriate times. Dandruff can be controlled with the proper conditioning and shampoo, including medicated shampoos for different scalp conditions. Consult your barber or stylist.

- <u>Split ends</u> result when there is not enough moisture and oil for softness or when hair is handled incorrectly. Split ends should be trimmed on a regular basis, usually every four to six weeks; otherwise the split continues upwards and result in additional breakage.

Hair Care

Regardless of the kind of hairstyle you choose, you need a good, consistent system for caring for your hair. It is just as important as a good skin-care system. Follow your hair care program on a regular basis, and be consistent for best results. Your program should consist of the following:

- <u>Shampoo</u>
  Shampoos come in varying strengths and for various purposes. Evaluate the type of hair you have and its condition, then choose a shampoo based on your specific needs. Do not use soap to shampoo your hair, because it leaves a residue that can cause hair to look flat and dull. Shampooing removes dead skin cells, oil, dirt, and odors from perspiration, fragrances and food. Make sure that you rinse thoroughly and choose a shampoo that will not dry out your hair. Check the pH balance of your shampoo; this will give you an idea of its balance between acidity and alkalinity

and help you decide what is right for your hair. If there is a beauty supply store in your area, shop there for greater variety.

- <u>Conditioner</u>

  There are many wonderful conditioners on the market today. A conditioner can help strengthen hair that has been damaged. It can make your hair more manageable, add body, make it appear more attractive, lustrous, and shiny. A conditioner is also good protection against ultraviolet rays.

- <u>Massage</u>

  A scalp massage is very beneficial and can help improve the health of your hair. It not only feels wonderful but also improves the health of your scalp and hair. It improves the blood circulation in your scalp, which helps because proper blood flow helps nourish hair. However, make sure that you do not pull your hair in the process, which can lead to breakage.

- <u>Hair loss</u>

  A certain amount of hair loss is natural—usually about 50 to 100 hairs daily. If you lose more than this on a continual basis, this could be a serious matter, and you should seek medical guidance. An unusual amount of hair loss is usually directly related to your health; if your body is unhealthy, your hair will be unhealthy. Poor diet is often a factor, such as if your metabolism is off. Toxins in the blood stream, anesthesia of any kind, shocks, drugs and severe emotional swings can cause excessive hair loss. Emotional or physical stress of any kind such as undergoing an operation, certain medications, depression, and pregnancy can all contribute to excessive hair loss. Again, if you experience ongoing hair loss as a result of any of these situations, seek medical help.

Tips on Hair Coloring

Coloring hair has become a fashion accessory, as well as a way to cover gray hair. However, you should always strive for a natural look when coloring your hair. Remember, everyone is born with a naturally balanced hair, eye, and skin pattern, and it is important to keep that balance when you color your hair. If you are unsure of the color range that is right for you, seek advice from someone with experience in this field. If your skin and eye coloring have warm, golden undertones, your choice of hair color should be variations of warm, gold or reddish colors. If you have cool, blue undertones in your skin and eye colors, go with variations of cool, ash golds or brown colors.

Your hair color should never clash with the color of your skin tone and eyes. If so, your hair will be calling for one color while your skin tone and eyes will need other colors for balance and symmetry—something will always seem off-balance. In order to color your hair correctly, become knowledgeable about the different kinds of coloring products that are available today:

- <u>Color rinses</u>
  These are temporary colors that coat the surface of the hair and wash out easily with the next shampoo. Color rinses provide gentle coloring and are less harsh on the hair than other processes. They are usually good for highlighting, adding shine, or enhancing natural coloring.

- Semi-permanent tints
  Semi-permanent colors give better coverage than rinses, especially on gray hair, and many may contain wonderful conditioning agents. They gradually wash out (usually between four and six washes with shampoo, but not necessarily completely). They usually brighten faded hair or give coverage to hair that is just beginning to gray. The coloring process is not as harsh on the hair as permanent coloring. Only color newly grown hair. Test the product as suggested, and follow instructions carefully.
- Permanent tinting
  These permanently change your hair color and hair structure. You must be careful when the hair grows out not to recolor the sections you already color processed—this can cause breakage, brittleness or ends with too much color concentration. Generally, only newly grown hair should be colored, and the rest of the hair and ends should be combed through with color according to the directions. Test the product first, usually 24 hours in advance, for allergic reactions. Avoid your eye area when using permanent tinting and always test it on your skin according to the directions. Be sure to check the brand that you will be using: many pictures on the color chart do not represent the true color of the product, and your hair can end up considerably darker than the color indicated, so choose your product accordingly. Also, the natural color of your hair will affect the final results. Avoid coloring your brows.

Whenever you color your hair, make sure you're using a good conditioner; this will help prevent hair breakage. It is also necessary to always follow the directions on the labels when coloring your hair. Do not take liberties with the product by adding your own ingredients or mixing contents in different proportions. If possible, it is better to get professional advice before coloring your hair, especially if you are going to be making permanent changes. A good hairstylist is not necessarily synonymous with a good colorist—professionals have different specialties.

If you are thinking of making a dramatic change in your hair color, you might want to try wearing a wig in that shade to see if you really like it. Today, there are many inexpensive, synthetic wigs available that you can purchase. It would be better to decide that you do not like a certain look or color before making any permanent changes to your own hair. Get feedback and opinions from close family members and friends. When hair is colored a very dark, even brown or black to cover up gray, this usually results in a single flat, solid color, which can be unattractive and aging as well as unnatural-looking. Try adding a few highlights in a slightly lighter shade for a more natural appearance, especially around the face, or choose a color that is a little lighter. Professional colorists are generally highly skilled in this area.

Chemical Relaxers

Chemical relaxers provide more freedom and flexibility of hairstyles, and they also help make your hair easier to manage. However, the price can be very high to your hair if it is not relaxed or cared for properly, as this process can cause damage, particularly hair loss or breakage. Familiarize yourself with different products because they vary in strength and results. Fine, medium, and very coarse hair need to be treated differently. If you are relaxing your own hair, study the directions carefully to find out what is best for you. When relaxing new growth, make sure that is the only area you are relaxing; otherwise, you might experience a lot of hair breakage. Always follow with a good conditioner, and conditioning on a regular basis is a must.

Important Tips for Relaxing Your Hair

- It is best to have your hair relaxed by a *professional.*
- Discuss coloring with the professional.
- Do not relax and color your hair at the same time.
- Do not relax your hair too often.
- A hot comb should never be used to touch up new growth.
- Make your hairdresser aware of any chemical products that you have used before.
- Avoid scratching your scalp.
- Do not exercise before relaxing your hair—acidic perspiration counteracts relaxers.

Curling Irons and Hot Combs

Curling irons provide flexibility in styling. They are quick and convenient, but they can dry your hair out, so always condition before you begin. It is usually best to make sure that your hair is dry before using a curling iron. Many people prefer blow drying. Hot combs can cause hair breakage if they are not used with caution. Always test for overheating. Excessive heat can burn your hair or scalp. Hair should be clean and completely dry. Light lubrication is desirable.

Blow-drying

Blow-drying is very good for drying hair quickly. Hair can also be styled and shaped simultaneously. Use a conditioner beforehand because of the amount of heat being applied to the hair. Try to blow-dry in moderation. Blow-drying helps add fullness if your hair is thin.

Permanents

Permanents allow for versatility and manageability, and they add body to limp and lifeless hair. However, a good haircut may be all that you need; choose what is right for your hair. Keep track of the products you are using on your hair, and try to be consistent. Read and reread instructions if you decide to perm your hair yourself. Avoid coloring your hair at the same time, and always consult a professional about when to recolor your hair and use a good conditioner. It is better to have a professional do this. A good conditioner is a must.

Baldness

Today, many men not only don't mind this look—they prefer it. The old stigma attached to baldness is becoming a thing of the past; the important thing about going bald is how it makes someone feel. If someone is self-accepting, warm and considerate of others, this is really what counts. On the other hand, if someone is insecure, ruthless, and selfish, this will affect how others relate to that person, whether bald or not. Poor disguises of a balding scalp undermine an otherwise positive image.

Hairpieces and Transplants

If going bald really bothers you, however, there are many wonderful, natural looking hairpieces on the market today. Just be sure that the hairpiece matches or blends with your natural hair coloring and texture. Also, choose a style that is natural looking for you—and pick a hairstyle that is comfortable.

If your hair is thinning, blow-drying can create a fuller effect. Your hairstylist may be helpful in recommending some haircuts or styles that can make your hair appear fuller. There are a number of new hair-care products on the market that can help to create a look of greater thickness. You might also want to look at the newer technologies in hair transplants. If you opt for a permanent change, make sure it is done by a highly recommended, certified, and experienced professional.

Hair Weaves, Extensions, and Braids

You can change your look completely if you desire to do so and create many different looks on a temporary basis with the use of hair weaves, extensions, and braids. Be careful to avoid damaging your hair by creating too much stress when using these hair accessories. There are professionals who are skilled in this area, and it is worth the money to seek their assistance.

Combing and Brushing

Combing and brushing your hair improperly can result in damaged hair. When combing, start from the ends and move up toward the scalp. You should never brush your hair while it is wet—this can cause your hair to break. Before combing, gently pat your hair dry with a towel or let it dry naturally. If your hair is tangled, do not pull it or tug at it because this will also cause breakage. Be gentle—this is a very important step in the care of your hair. Never rub your hair vigorously when it is wet. Always comb your hair in small sections and use a natural bristle brush.

8

Attention: All Faces

Your face is often the first thing that people notice about you. Everything else about you plays an important role in your first impression, but it is your face that is typically the initial point of interest. Therefore, give your face the time and attention that it deserves!

There are no unattractive people in the world; there is something beautiful and attractive about everyone. This is remarkable, when you think about it: No one will ever smile, laugh or look exactly the way that you do; no one will be able to communicate things quite the way that you do with your smile, your eyes, and your expressions. So why not make the most of your face? There are many things that you can do to enhance your individual gift.

Your Face Shape

Start by analyzing the shape of your face. This will determine your best hairstyle and shape of your glasses. For men, the style or type of beard or moustache that is most flattering is determined by your face shape. For women, your face shape determines the placement of makeup. All of these choices should compliment your best facial features and play down the ones that you feel are less flattering. There are seven distinct face shapes:

<u>Oval:</u> This is considered the most perfectly balanced face. The proportions have the greatest balance of all of the face shapes.

<u>Round:</u> This face is curved in shape; there are not many angles at the chin, forehead, and brows. The cheekbones are usually broad and the face has almost the same length as width.

<u>Diamond:</u> The cheek area is widest with tapering at the forehead and chin.

<u>Heart:</u> There is broadness at the forehead with a gradual tapering to a narrow chin.

<u>Rectangle:</u> This face is much longer than wider with straight sides. It may or may not have sharp angles.

<u>Triangle (or pear):</u> There is more fullness in the jaw line than at the forehead.

Square: The fullness in the forehead is the same as in the jawline and cheeks. The angles are more defined in the forehead and jawline.

Once again, please remember that every face is an attractive face.

Choosing the Right Hairstyle

The hairstyle that you select should call attention to your best facial features and play down your least favorite features. Your hairstyle is very important in providing balance to your face. It should also be appropriate for your lifestyle, personality, body line and proportions, face shape, size and type of hair.

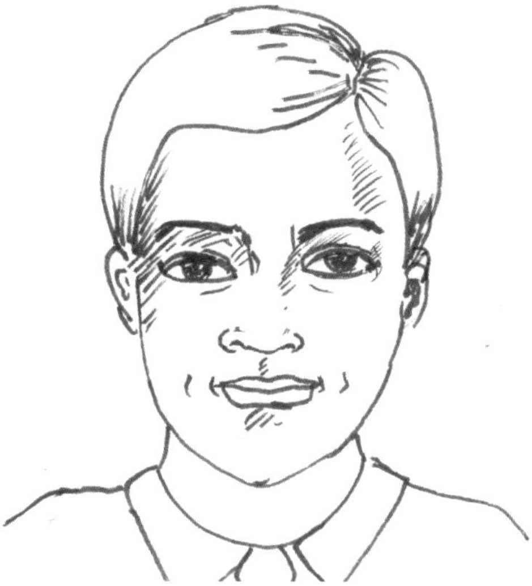

MAN

WOMAN

OVAL

This face is well-proportioned. The forehead is slightly wider than the chin or cheeks. A person with an oval face and regular features can wear many different styles. Most styles are flattering to you; however, your hairstyle should be in balance with the size of your face. Hair combed off the face can be very becoming but, some faces may require a softer look. Do not cover up your face with too much hair if your face is small. Your hair can be worn long or short. A part in your hair is optional.

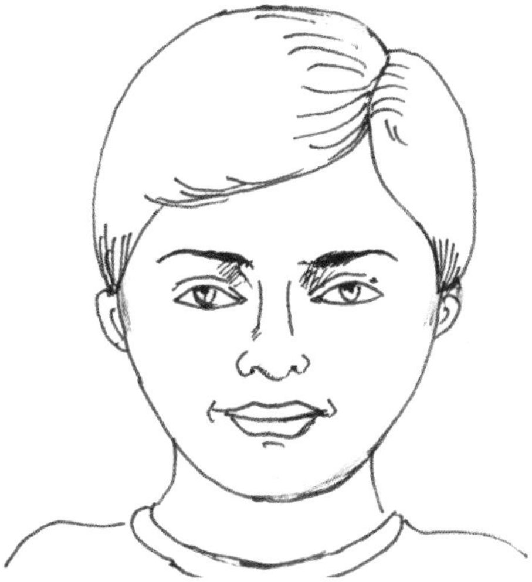

MAN WOMAN

ROUND

The round-shaped face is one of curves. It is about the same in length as it is in width. Hair should be kept closer to the sides of the face and a center part should be avoided. Place fullness in the upper third of the face above the cheek bones. Try to elongate your face with your hairstyle. Aim for more height rather than width so that length and height balance out. Avoid fullness at the jaw line as well as hair worn pulled back. Choose an off-centered part or hairstyle.

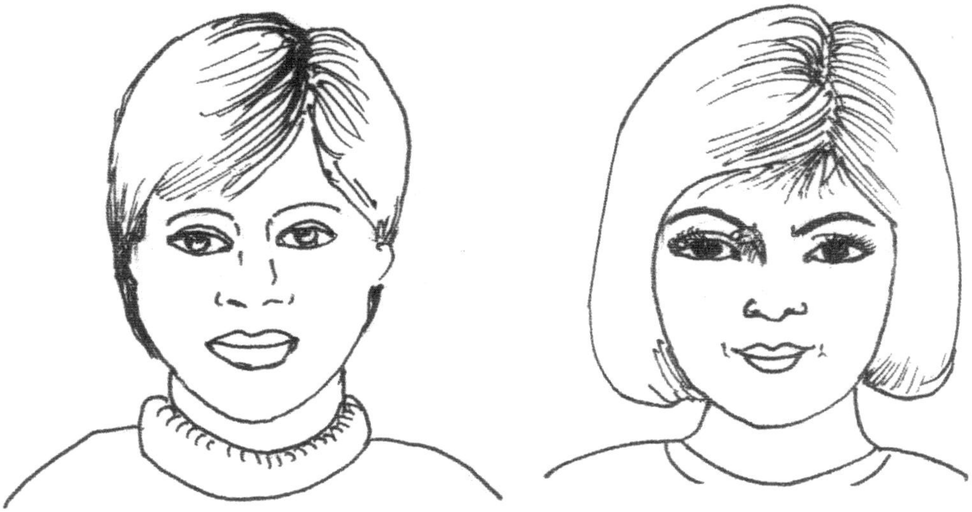

MAN WOMAN

DIAMOND

A diamond-shaped face is characterized by more width at the cheekbones. The forehead and chin are narrow in comparison. Lift the hair to frame the broadness in the cheekbones. This balances the forehead and jaws with the cheeks. Add fullness at the jaw line to fill out a narrow chin and at the forehead. You can use an off-center part and bangs. Do not wear your hair too high and avoid fullness at the widest part. Create width at the forehead when possible.

MAN

WOMAN

HEART

You can wear hair longer, looser, and fuller. Balance the full forehead and narrow chin with more fullness near the chin area. Always choose an off-center part, and avoid too much fullness near the temples and on top. Bangs worn to the side work well for you. For men, a beard can balance a narrow chin. Fullness can be added at the back of the neck.

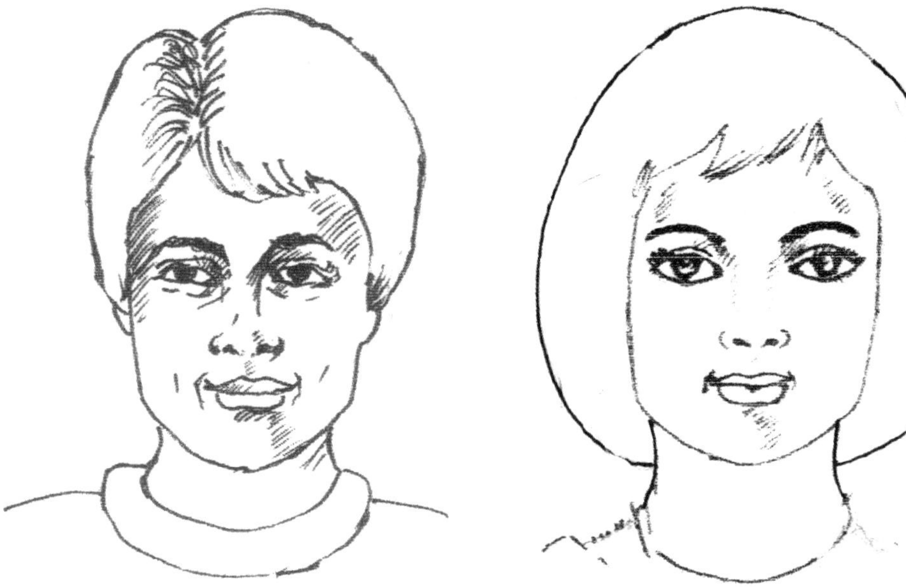

MAN WOMAN

RECTANGLE

This face has more length than width. Avoid a center part and too much height. Off-center bangs can be very flattering. Hair should be fullest at the temple and fuller at the sides with an off-center part. Wear short to medium length styles. For men, extending the sideburns to just below the ears can help to minimize the length of the face. To balance a square jaw line, avoid long, straight hair, which can add length to the face.

MAN

WOMAN

TRIANGLE (Pear)

Avoid placing fullness at the cheek and jaw area. Strive for fullness at the crown of the head instead, and create softness and fullness at the forehead. Avoid styles that stop right at the jaw line because this emphasizes the fullness in that area. An off-center part or bangs can be flattering. Avoid pulling hair back in a severe style.

MAN WOMAN

SQUARE

Wear an off-center part and use height and roundness at the sides to create the illusion of curves and balance. A square-shaped face has about as much length as it has width; it can have an angular or square chin or forehead. Add roundness in the hair near the jawline, and soften your face angles. Keep the lines soft and varied; avoid wearing straight bangs, a squared line at the jaw, and sharp angles in general. Curved bangs are best. Sideburns should be a little longer than usual. Create softness, curls, and soft waves at the forehead. Strive to add the illusion of length to the face.

Glasses

Glasses are practical and functional—but are also terrific fashion accessories that can help make you look more attractive. Today, when you go to buy glasses, many workers are trained to help you select frames that are attractive and flattering as well as practical. In particular, keep your hairstyle in mind while choosing glasses. The shape and size of your glasses should flatter your face and features. They should also reflect your personality and match your lifestyle. Your glasses should not overshadow you, whether socially or at work.

The color of your frames should blend with your eyes, skin tone, and especially your hair color. Your frames should also compliment your overall choice of color in your clothing and other accessories. If you choose glasses in a metal frame, choose gold if you look best in warm colors such as oranges, corals, yellows and browns; choose silver if you look best in cool colors such as blues, purples, and grays.

Sunglasses

If you need to wear glasses on a regular basis, it is neither practical nor desirable to combine your glasses and sunglasses. People find it difficult to relate to or establish contact with a person whose eyes they can never see.

Contact Lenses

Contact lenses are a good alternative to regular glasses, and your choice between the two is entirely personal. Contact lenses are very convenient for people who are physically active. If you like wearing them on a regular basis, it is good to give your eyes a rest from time to time. If you decide to wear colored contacts, make sure that the color you choose does not clash with your own natural hair and skin coloring.

Note: Remember to keep your individual face shape in mind while selecting a pair of glasses.

MAN WOMAN

OVAL

A person with an oval-shaped face has a great variety of choices in eyewear. However, let your choice harmonize with your body, face, personality, and lifestyle. If you are conservative in lifestyle or character, do not choose anything too outrageous unless you can afford an extra pair of glasses for occasional fun wear.

MAN

WOMAN

ROUND

In order to create a balance, do not go to the opposite extreme and choose extremely square frames—this will create too much contrast. Avoid round-shaped glasses, too. Choose glasses that will help to create some angles; you can choose glasses that are square or rectangular but softly rounded.

MAN

WOMAN

DIAMOND

Your goal is to add width in both the chin and forehead areas. Select frames that draw attention away from the cheekbones in order to create this balance.

MAN WOMAN

HEART

The goal is to balance the broadness of the forehead with the narrowness of the chin. Avoid heaviness at the top of the frames. Frames should not extend beyond your temples. Avoid square frames.

MAN

WOMAN

RECTANGLE

Choose frames that create roundness at the temples and at eye level. The frames should have some width and roundness to them if your face has sharp angles. A square frame that is slightly rounded and wide is a good choice if you have roundness in the face. You can also add some angles in your glasses.

MAN

WOMAN

TRIANGLE (Pear-Shaped)

Choose glasses that will call attention to the upper portion of your face—the right pair will draw eyes away from the fullness in the jaw area. Balance is created between the upper and the lower parts of your face.

MAN WOMAN

SQUARE

If you want to soften the squareness and angles of your face and create curves, avoid square or sharply angled glasses. You can choose a rounded, slightly curved, square frame. A softly rounded frame is also a good choice.

Moustaches

Your moustache, like your hairstyle, should be appropriate for your lifestyle and should flatter the shape of your face. Exaggerated shapes in a moustache can give a very sinister or frivolous appearance, which can detract from your overall credibility and desired image. Your moustache should always be well groomed and trimmed on a regular basis. A moustache can emphasize your more attractive features; it can also help to downplay less attractive features by drawing attention away from them.

Beards

Your beard should flatter the shape of your face and features and should be suitable for your lifestyle. Your barber or stylist can be very helpful in determining the best shape for you. Some men are much more attractive in a small, neat beard and moustache. Keep in mind that a beard might not be appropriate for your particular line of work—in some conservative circles or business situations, even well-trimmed beards are considered to be generally unacceptable. It can detract from what you wish to project. Bushy beards can take away from your appearance and credibility and create a lack of concentration by others on what you are actually saying or doing.

Plastic Surgery

If you are interested in plastic surgery, get as much information as possible about the procedures that appeal to you. You should also investigate the doctor's background and qualifications thoroughly. It is a good idea to request recommendations from past patients. Have consultations with several physicians. It is neither a badge of shame nor a badge of honor to have plastic surgery. What counts is ultimately how it makes you feel about yourself. But remember: Plastic surgery is not a substitute for positive self-esteem. It is not necessary to discuss it one way or another with other people. What people do in the privacy of beauty salons, medical centers, or their homes to enhance their appearances is a personal choice—and the same applies to you.

9

Makeup

Stand Up and Stand Out

Makeup is fun and functional. It is an extension of your clothing and accessories. It gives your skin a finished, polished look. Some use of makeup shows that you have taken time and care to do the best that you can with your appearance. However, heavy makeup won't conceal skin that hasn't been properly cared for due to poor diet, lack of exercise, insufficient rest, or improper cleansing—this will only contribute to the problem. Makeup should make your skin look and feel better, but it should always look natural. Use makeup to emphasize your most attractive features and to play down the features that do not satisfy you.

Your makeup should enhance your overall look. It should always reflect you and be appropriate to the time and place. Check new trends for ideas and products that may be helpful to you. Do not use anything just because it is trendy, unless it helps you to look more attractive. The colors of the makeup you choose are very important. They should harmonize with—but not necessarily match—the colors of your clothing, eyes, hair, and skin. Also consider your personality, age, lifestyle, and what is generally flattering to you.

Make sure that your foundation, eye makeup, blush and lipstick are in the same color range (warm or cool) and blend with each other. There are some neutral reds that will work with both warm and cool tones. Look for cosmetic kits color-coordinated for warm or cool skin tones—this takes the guesswork out of makeup. Be careful of fluorescent lighting when shopping for makeup: It will affect how the colors appear on you. Your makeup for day should be more subtle; add more for evening wear if desired.

Serums and Primers

Serums and primers are the new kids on the block: Both support and enhance the work of your other skin-care products and makeup. Serums are applied before moisturizers, and primers are applied before putting on foundations. They help foundations glide on more smoothly and prevent them from settling into fine lines and creases, diminishing their appearance.

Foundation

Foundations have become multi-faceted. Some have built-in skin treatments. Even if you do not really need foundation, it helps your makeup and blush glide on more easily and blend better. Foundation serves as an additional protective layer over your moisturizer. It can balance ruddiness or sallowness as well as minimize flaws.

Make sure that your skin is clean and moisturized before you apply foundation. Apply your foundation while your moisturizer is still slightly damp for a soft, smooth look. There are some wonderful moisturizer and foundation combinations available today.

Choose a foundation as close to your natural coloring as possible. You might have to blend a couple of shades to get the right color. Test along your jaw line. Apply your foundation in dots sparingly and blend well with clean fingers or a damp makeup sponge. Blend your foundation well and evenly into your jaw line, outward and upward into the hairline. Your choice of a foundation is determined by your skin type.

- If you have normal to dry skin, use a foundation that will protect your skin from further dryness and will help your skin to hold onto its natural moisture.
- People with combination and oily skin should use a foundation that will help to absorb excessive oil and discourage shine without having a drying effect on your skin. Large pores will also be minimized.

Eyes

The eyes are often referred to as the windows to the soul. They might be described as your most attractive and expressive feature, and they should definitely be enhanced. Your eyes tell a lot about you, so it is only natural to try to make them as attractive as possible. When applying any kind of makeup, pat outward on the upper lid and inward under the eye with your ring finger. Be careful not to pull the eyelids when applying makeup. Choose colors that harmonize with your eye color.

Eyebrows

Your eyebrows create an attractive frame for your eyes. They give your eyes added expression. Brush your brows up and then out using an eyebrow brush or a brow fix. Then follow their natural shape if you have an attractive brow line. Use a brow pencil or shadow in short, feathered strokes to shape and fill in your eyebrows. Always use a brush afterwards for final blending. Do not use a solid line when filling in your eyebrows because this creates a very harsh look. Remove straggly hairs following your natural line prior to shaping and filling in your brows with your pencil or powder. Your eyebrows should be the same color as your hair or at least close to it. If your hair is medium to light in color, black gives a very harsh look; softer tones look much more natural. Your eyebrows should not be too severe in appearance. Different shapes come and go in fashion but be aware of how different shapes affect you. Keep in mind the following:

- Very thin eyebrows can create a severe look.
- Eyebrows arched down to the temple give a sad, anxious, outdated look.
- Thick and bushy eyebrows present a sloppy and unkempt appearance.

Eye Shadow

Always use eye shadow to flatter the shape of your eyes. Eye shadow brings out the color of your eyes and makes your eyes seem larger and more attractive. Eye shadows come in different forms. Experiment to find out what works best for you. Be wary of frosted shadows because they can sometimes emphasize lines and create an unattractive, creepy look. Blending is the key to all makeup, and this is especially important for the eyes. If more than one color is used, blend them all together for a natural look. Choose colors that emphasize your eyes but do not take over. Always use a brush for blending.

Eyeliner

Eyeliner adds dimension to the shape of your eyes—it adds depth and emphasizes your lashes. Eyeliner makes your eyes more attractive, but it should not be too harshly applied. Subtlety is the key: Use a color that does not become the focal point of your face unless you are doing it on purpose for a particular effect. Once you've put it on, step back and see if it actually is flattering.

Whatever your choice, blend well. A soft brush can be used for blending in order to create a more natural look. Apply eyeliner as close to your lash lines as possible. A pencil or cream eyeliner usually glides on more smoothly than a liquid eyeliner; a liquid eyeliner requires more control. If eyeliner is applied on the lower lid, it should be softly done and blended well. Eyeliner on the lower lid can be aging and create a harsh look if applied too heavily. Apply and blend eyeliner before applying shadow, then blend them together for a more natural look.

Lipstick and Lip Gloss

Lipstick and lip gloss unify the upper portion and lower part of your face for a balanced look. Lipstick should complement your cheek color in tone and intensity for a strong overall effect. Make sure that the colors do not clash. Both should complement your eye color as well as the color in your clothing. Always outline your lips with a pencil first (lip liner). Avoid too much contrast. Start at one side of the top lip from the center and work outward, then repeat on the other side. Then, start from the outside working inward to the center for each side on the bottom lip. Fill in with your lipstick and always use a lipstick brush for a better look. For the illusion of fuller lips, place lip pencil lines outside your natural lip line. To create thinner lips, place the line inside your natural line. Experiment with different colors, but keep the lip pencil color near the lipstick color. Your choice of colors and intensity may be different for daytime than for the evening. Lip glosses can be used alone or with lipstick.

Face Powder

Your face powder provides a special touch to makeup. It evens out your skin tone and gives your skin a nice, finished surface. Use powder after you have applied your foundation and cream blush. Eye makeup, lipstick, and powder blush should be applied after powder. A translucent powder will not alter the color of the rest of your makeup. Never rub powder into your skin. Apply it with a puff, cotton ball, brush or sponge stroking downward. Too much powder can emphasize creases and lines so be careful of the eye area and remove all loose powder. Use your powder brush to remove excess powder for a natural look.

<u>Benefits of powder:</u>

- It balances and absorbs oil.
- It controls shine.
- It helps set your makeup so that it lasts longer.

Blush

Your blush should always look natural and give you a healthy look. Always apply sparingly. A cream blush is good for dry skin and can serve as a good undercoat for a powder blush; if you try this, apply cream blush first, then face powder, and then add powder blush for added coverage. Blend well and use similar tones.

Powder blushes are easier to use and work well for normal or oily skin. Always use a brush for blending. When applying your blush, define your cheekbone area and blend well into the hairline. Never go beyond the midpoint of the eye, moving outward towards the ear, and do not place your blush lower than the tip of your nose. Remember: Less is more. Avoid blobs and streaks of color by blending well. Blushes come in cool or warm tones and should harmonize with the rest of your makeup colors.

Mascara

Different kinds of mascara perform different functions. There are mascaras for lengthening, thickening, and darkening your lashes. There are also waterproof mascaras. If you are using more than one coat, let the first one dry before applying a second coat. Mascara completes your eye makeup and helps define the shape of your eyes. However, it should not change the color of your lashes (unless your lashes are very pale); it should only enhance them. Neutral colors are better—black, charcoal, or brown, in a shade that is right for you. Contrasting colors on your lashes can be overly distracting. However, for a festive occasion, a different color can be fun.

Removing waterproof mascara can be difficult—it can cause you to pull the skin around the eyes and cause stretching in the process. Use a remover designed for waterproof mascara.

Highlighters and Concealers

Highlighters and concealers can help you emphasize your best features and play down the features you do not like. Light colors emphasize or call attention to a particular area. Dark colors cause areas to recede or deepen. Highlighters and concealers should be used sparingly and blended very well with your foundation for a natural look.

Nail Polish

Well-groomed and nicely polished nails give a wonderful, finished look to your appearance because your hands and nails are constantly in view. Avoid a very bizarre color or excessively long nails for day wear. There are many lovely coordinated lip and nail colors available today.

Care of Makeup

Always make sure that your hands are clean before putting on makeup. Avoid storing your makeup in a place with extreme temperatures. Also avoid dampness or excessive humidity. Do not place your cosmetics in direct sunlight.

Use disposable cotton pads or balls and cotton tips when possible, and toss them after one use. If you use sponges, keep them clean. Close the makeup containers tightly to avoid drying and to keep out germs. Go through your cosmetics on a regular basis and eliminate those that you no longer use or those that have dried out. Replace dated cosmetics on a regular basis as well. This will also enable you to be more familiar with your products. You can then be more creative and try color combinations that you never thought of using before.

Clean your brushes on a regular basis. Wash them out with a mild detergent and warm water and then rinse; pat gently with a terry-cloth towel, and allow the brushes to dry before storing them.

Part II

Program Yourself for Success

10

Those Other Things that Mean So Much

Once you are satisfied with how you look, turn your attention to other things that are equally important. Together, all of these elements help you find the right balance that you need in your life.

Relaxation

Relaxation is a gift that you give to yourself. Even with the busiest schedule, it is important to carve out some time to relax. It does not have to be for an extended period of time; even a short period of time will make a difference. Allowing yourself time to relax will actually enable you to be more productive. You will feel physically restored and mentally and emotionally uplifted. It is also a great stress-buster.

Try different forms of relaxation until you find the one that works best for you. However, keep in mind that what relaxes your friends or significant other may not be right for you. Some popular forms of relaxation are listening to quiet music, taking a soothing bath, reading, meditating and exercising. Also, a good massage can work wonders.

Sleep

The amount of sleep each person needs varies, but a refreshing night's sleep can set the tone for your entire day. You will definitely feel better, and it can help you think more clearly and sharply. You should be able to accomplish more in less time. When you have had enough sleep, you don't only feel better—you look better, too. Sleep has long been identified as one of the great friends of beauty and attractiveness—after all, it isn't called "beauty sleep" for nothing. The amount of sleep needed varies with each individual.

The Importance of Your Home

Your home is a great anchor for you. In today's hectic world of stress and tension, it is necessary to have a home that balances and supports your life in the outside world. No matter what is going on in the outside world, you should be able to walk into your home, unwind, begin relaxing and find your balance. If a home is cluttered, untidy, and disorganized, it will not offer the relaxation, balance, and renewal that is so essential for today.

The colors that you choose in your home can greatly affect your ability to feel rested, at ease, and peaceful there. Colors that you look for in clothing are not necessarily the same colors that you may want in your living space—you might look best in vibrant, intense colors, but while you may enjoy wearing these colors, you might prefer more quiet, softer and soothing, restful variations of them for your home. The opposite is also true. Your home should allow you to relax and renew yourself and prepare you to face the outside world again. Pay special attention to your bedroom. Today, many bedrooms function as all-purpose rooms—a place to eat, work, and sleep—and all of this activity can rob it of its relaxing atmosphere if not carefully done.

Time Management

Time management is necessary to combat stress and procrastination. Manage your time so that you can finish tasks that you have started in a realistic way and then allow time for yourself. Do not let other people make unrealistic demands on your time. This only leads to resentment and anger building up inside you, only to explode later. Do not overcommit yourself, either to your job or at home, because in the end, everyone suffers. Learn how to say no to unrealistic time schedules and demands without feeling guilty.

Organization

You will make your life so much easier if you are organized. You will spend less time looking for misplaced items or doing the same tasks over and over. Lack of organization results in a tremendous loss of time and energy. It can make you feel very frustrated and it encourages procrastination. If you always have to get organized before you start any project or task, this will detract from your actual productivity. You will feel more productive if you are able to start your task or project right away.

If you have a history of being disorganized, make a promise to yourself to do something about it today. Do not try to organize everything at once. Start at home by organizing one thing or room at a time. Keep it simple, such as organizing your shirts and ties or your scarves and makeup. Slowly, but surely, your whole closet will become organized. Maintain a steady pace of organization, and before you know it, you will have a whole room organized and eventually your entire home or garage. You can also do this at work. Start by organizing your desktop, then one drawer at a time. Do the same for your records and files. You will experience a wonderful feeling of satisfaction and accomplishment.

Procrastination

Procrastination is a tremendous financial, physical, and emotional drain. It is a ruthless companion that saps time, strength, and energy. Sometimes procrastination occurs as a result of setting unrealistic goals—trying to accomplish too many goals in an unrealistic timeframe. You might not be equipped or qualified for what you are trying to do at this particular time and sometimes when you do not know where or how to start a project, you do nothing at all. When this happens, overcome your delaying by breaking down the project at hand into smaller projects. Do one thing at a time. Small tasks, finished one by one, will lead to the completion of a bigger task.

When you ask too much of yourself in an unrealistic situation, you often become immobilized. Frustration builds up, and you end up not accomplishing anything. The telephone, the television, and daydreams become great allies, but you do not really enjoy these either because your task is still hanging over your head. It becomes a vicious cycle of avoidance and worry. Try not to get yourself into such a situation in the first place.

Challenges

Be willing to stretch your horizons and try something new. Be willing to take reasonable risks and to be challenged, and try to be more accepting of a situation that does not work out well. Failure is never the end of the world. No matter what happens, you will learn from the experience. Do not allow yourself to be held back by fear or anxiety. If you fail at something, do not continue to dwell on the failure. Assess the situation; think about what happened and how you responded. Think about what you would change and what you would do differently. Put it aside and be willing to move forward. Do not let a setback immobilize you. Remember, out of every negative situation, some good can come.

Stress

Many of today's diseases are stress-related. Stress can tax you physically, emotionally, and mentally. It can affect the way you look, feel, and function. A certain amount of stress is healthy but you have to listen to your body and learn the difference between what is healthy for you and what is unhealthy. Some people thrive on a lot of stress, but for other people much less stress can be overwhelming. The demands and stresses of simple, everyday life create their own levels of challenge. You cannot avoid stress entirely, however—whether you are excited or anxious, happy or sad, a certain amount of stress is created.

When processed properly, a certain amount of stress can help you be productive and creative and accomplish necessary goals. This is the healthy side of stress. However, after a stressful situation, your body usually knows how to let go, wind down and balance itself out—it is unhealthy when stress is ongoing and unrelenting.

When stress occurs, you need to try to pinpoint the cause of your stress. Ask yourself if your goals are unrealistic. It will not be the end of the world if you do not get what you want when you want it, such as a promotion at work. As another example, it is better to have to go to night school one more semester than have an overloaded schedule after working a strenuous job all day. Perhaps you are too hard on yourself in general. Stop making unnecessary demands on yourself; step back and think about whether you are happy and whether changes in your life (such as in your career or in romance) might be beneficial.

<u>There are many effective ways of coping with stress:</u>

- Exercise regularly—working out in moderation can reduce stress buildup.
- Balance your activities—if you are planning to do more than you can realistically handle, rethink your schedule.
- Avoid excessive pressure, internally and externally.
- Set priorities—allow time for yourself. Set yourself time limits for certain tasks.
- Allow yourself enough time to relax.
- Balance your diet—excessive sugar and fats, caffeine, alcohol and other stimulants will only increase your stress level.

- Avoid procrastination—it goes hand-in-hand with stress.
- Delegate tasks.
- Find time to laugh.

Letting Go

At the end of the day, try to calm yourself down and let go of everything. Do not keep replaying portions of the day over and over in your mind such as a disagreement with someone or a job interview that you wish you had handled differently. Try to realize that you cannot do any more about it today—you were doing the best that you could at the time. Know that tomorrow is another day and vow to be and do the best that you can at that time. Then give yourself a restful, well-deserved night of sleep.

11

Say What You Mean:
Verbal and Nonverbal Communication

Communication, both verbal and nonverbal, is always taking place. Many people feel comfortable with what they know and who they are, but they do not spend enough time and attention in getting this across to other people. Your body language, facial expressions and general appearance reflect how you think and feel, and both verbal and nonverbal communication make a definite statement about you—whether you want it to or not—so make them work to your advantage. They can help people become interested in learning more about you. It can take people's opinions of you out of neutral and project a positive impression of you. As you will see, this is a lesson that Dan learned the hard way.

> *Dan is now one of the most successful salesmen in his region. Other salesmen in his office look at him in awe and with a great deal of respect. He has come a long way in the last eight years. Sometimes he thinks about the early years and smiles. He would rush in to see potential customers because he wanted to let them know about his great product. He was rigid and tense. His days were long and frustrating. He seldom sold anything.*
>
> *Five years ago, Dan discovered the secret of selling himself before he attempted to sell his product. Now he takes the time to relax and relate to his potential customers. They might talk about quite a few things before they discuss his product. His manner is relaxed, sincere, and friendly. He relays trust and confidence in his verbal and nonverbal communication. His customers feel that they can trust his product, too. They are very loyal and they also tell their friends about him.*

As Dan learned, you tell a story about yourself in the way in which you use your hands, arms, and eyes; in your facial expression; even in the ways you sit, stand, and walk. Your verbal expression—the tone and pitch of your voice—influences this story, either positively or negatively. Your nonverbal communication should support what you are verbally trying to get across.

Try to determine the appropriate communication for the occasion at hand as soon as possible. Look at what is going on around you and take your cue from that. Communicating and relating at a job interview should be a little more reserved than usual but not too aloof. A friendly get-together should be more relaxed.

Verbal Communication

When speaking, avoid a tentative manner. If you do not project belief in what you are saying or doing, it will make it difficult for other people to believe in you, too. Be sincere. Project authority—but not harshness—when you communicate with others. Let your smile work for you; it should be genuine and sincere and should not come across as patronizing or forced. Voice and gestures should be in agreement.

Voice

Your voice affects how listeners perceive you. It also lets other people know your feelings about yourself and others. A tape recorder is an excellent tool for making voice improvements. To use your voice effectively, consider the following:

- Speaking softly can indicate a lack of self-confidence or of conviction in what you are saying. However, avoid going overboard with an aggressive voice. Speak up so that you can be heard, but do not yell.
- Be aware of speaking in a voice that whines, barks, or is too shrill. It is very distracting. This can indicate low self-esteem and a lack of self-confidence.

- Watch for the appropriate inflection in your tone. A statement should not lift to an inappropriate question or fall away at the end.
- Always pronounce your words clearly.
- Watch out for prefacing a sentence with an apology just in case you make a mistake.
- Talking too much can be a clear indication of nervousness, insensitivity or aggressiveness.
- The use of slang or cute words is fine for a social situation with friends but not for work or business meetings.
- Stumbling through countless "umms" and "uhs" in your speech can be very distracting.
- Do not begin a sentence, stop in midstream and then start another sentence or thought before finishing the first one. Do not leave sentences dangling.
- Run-on sentences are confusing to the listener, and you can never tell where one thought ends and another begins; they can suggest disorganization and confusion as well as a lack of focus.
- Answering a question with a question should be avoided. Try to pause and listen to what is being asked of you rather than rushing headlong into another question.
- Nod and smile when appropriate but not continually.
- Be conscious of your facial expression and match it to what you are saying.
- Project power and authority in the way you communicate, but do it with

subtlety and without harshness.

Telephone Communication Skills

Communicating by telephone is a part of everyday life, so developing good phone conversation skills is essential. You often have to rely on the telephone to make a good first impression. When using the telephone, use these tips:

- Talk directly into the telephone.
- Do not eat while you are on the phone and turn off any distracting music.
- Smile into the phone and sit up straight. You will sound more positive and pleasant.
- Do not fiddle with anything that creates distracting background noises while you are attempting to talk.
- Identify yourself and your company or organization immediately. Explain why you are calling.
- Make your voice interesting but not aggressive.
- Be courteous and speak clearly.
- Place calls at convenient and reasonable times.
- Avoid interrupting, and be a good listener.
- Do not keep other people waiting on the phone while you have extensive conversations with others. Everyone's time is valuable.
- Choose words that have a clear meaning. Jot down what you want to say.

Nonverbal Communication

Once you see what is appropriate in a situation, handle yourself accordingly but also add your own personal touch. Always let the real you shine through in a positive, genuine way.

- A handshake should be firm but not brutal or aggressive. It should not be limp, passive, or wimpy. Clean hands and well-groomed nails will stand out on these occasions.
- Your posture can enhance or detract from your overall appearance. It can suggest confidence and poise—or indecisiveness, uncertainty, and low self-esteem. How you sit, stand, and move reveals a wealth of information about you. Avoid the appearance of studying the floor or the ceiling when someone is addressing you.
- Walking too hurriedly or too sluggishly sends out negative signals about you. Look in a mirror or store window as you pass to make sure that you do not appear too lethargic or too wound up. Evaluate your movements. Do not amble along or speed by; try an evenly paced, purposeful stride.

If you are not satisfied with your posture or how you walk after observing yourself in a mirror, take steps to do something about it. You can practice when you are alone at home. The goal is to appear graceful and relaxed; hold your head erect and your upper body balanced. Do not hold your shoulders and head too rigidly. Be aware of the position of your legs, especially if you cross them when sitting. It can make the difference between looking graceful or awkward.

Do not slouch or crouch down in your seat. You will get the hang of it as you practice.

Do's and Don'ts in Nonverbal Communication

- Placing your hand over your mouth and dropping your head can indicate indecisiveness and uncertainty. People will tend to concentrate on your gestures rather than on what you are saying.
- Excessive nodding eliminates the opportunity of being included in the conversation. It can also be a sign of insecurity.
- Too many hand gestures can be distracting. Tugging at your rings, earrings, necktie, moustache, beard, or hair can indicate nervousness and a lack of confidence. Try to keep your hands relaxed.

Facial Expressions

Your facial expression supplies visual information that supports or negates your verbal message. It tells people what you are thinking and feeling. A severe, glum, blank, or hollow expression will not attract people to you. Conversely, a naturally warm, confident, friendly, interested, and pleasant expression will draw people to you.

> *Roberta was involved in a project that required a lot of planning and months of preparation. It was to culminate with a big program one evening. A lot of people worked very hard to make the event successful.*
>
> *Roberta and an associate were making final preparations*

for the program that evening. A man who had not been involved at all came up to them and began bitterly attacking the way that everything was being handled. They tried to explain why things were being done this way. After spewing out other criticisms and very negative commands, the man left.

Roberta's associate congratulated her on how she had handled the situation. Roberta responded, "To tell you the truth, I was too stunned to do very much." She said that she had been amazed as she watched this person's facial expression change. He took on an increasingly unattractive and distorted look as he poured out all of his negativity, until he was hardly recognizable.

When you have a positive attitude, it radiates out to everything around you, and that will say more for you than anything that you can say in words.

Eye Contact

Your eyes help to carry the meaning of your words. While eye contact is important, you should not stare. Too much eye contact can cause discomfort. Appropriate eye contact establishes a positive bond with an individual or group.

Job Interviews

Relax and project what is special about you. It is not necessary to boast or try too hard to make yourself look good. Present your background and qualifications in an orderly, modest manner. Never get too personal.

Be yourself and always end on a positive note. Smile pleasantly when appropriate. Concentrate on your uniqueness and show how it will benefit your potential employer to hire you. Let your special talents, skills, and abilites be acknowledged. Do not concentrate on your shortcomings. If you are nervous, take a deep breath before asking a question or answering it. Concentrate on what is being said or asked of you.

Some job interview tips:

- Be neatly dressed and well groomed.
- Hair should be neatly cut—eccentric hairstyles should be avoided.
- Bring a good pen that is not dried up or out of ink.
- Bring necessary documents, such as your Social Security card and your résumé with references.
- Fill your work application out neatly and completely.
- Do not keep looking at your watch or at the clock on the wall.
- Do not smoke or chew gum.
- Be familiar with the company beforehand.
- Ask in an interested manner about your potential employer and job expectations.
- Find out what the job duties are, and be interested in what is going on around you.
- Be sincere in your manner.

Recently James, a career counselor, talked with a client who had just finished college and was looking for a job. The client, Bob, was a physical education major who was hoping to get a job as a physical education instructor in a high school. He admitted that he was having problems with his interviewing skills. Bob felt that he had everything that was needed in order to be a good teacher. He felt that he was intelligent, he kept himself in good shape and he had a good personality. However, Bob recognized that he was defensive when he went into an interview.

James tried to help him understand that the person on the other side of the desk had a lot of responsibility. If Bob could just put himself in that person's place he would be less defensive. The interviewer was charged with making the right judgment in order to choose the right teacher. The right teacher had to fit in with the students and with the school, had to adhere to the proper dress code, and had to do all of the things required of a good teacher. Now, think of the person in that position. What if he made the wrong decision? What would that mean for him? Would it mean a reprimand? Would it mean his job? The interviewer himself was also under a large amount of pressure.

So James asked Bob to be himself, to try to answer the questions as best he could and to think about why the person interviewing him was asking these questions. He told Bob to try to have some empathy for that person. In this way, Bob would find that he could be much less defensive and more relaxed.

When Bob went to an interview, James asked him to hold

good thoughts, to be positive and to remember that the right job was seeking him just as he was seeking the right job.

No job interview is ever a waste, whether or not you get the job. Even if you are not hired, the important thing is that you had the courage to try. Take a few minutes to jot down notes on what went well and also on what you could have done differently.

Résumés

A good résumé is essential. It is your calling card. It serves a twofold purpose: Your résumé is your initial way of introducing yourself, and it also should pique positive interest in you. It motivates someone to want to meet you or know more about you. It also provides an opportunity for you to get your foot in the door. A good résumé can help you to get an interview, and it can help you during an interview. It can also work for you afterward, leaving a favorable impression.

A good résumé is an investment in yourself and your future. Always check your spelling and always use a simple, easy-to-follow layout. Choose good quality paper. Remember to include all of your qualifications and credentials. It is also helpful to jot these down beforehand so that you don't leave anything important out. There are people who specialize in this service. If you cannot afford such a service, enlist the help of your family and friends.

Presentation Pointers

- Research and organize your material. Prepare well ahead of time.

Practice your presentation as well as your introductory statements.

- Practice your body language to make sure it matches what you are saying. You are always being observed.
- Use language that is appropriate; using a lot of large words when they're not required can turn off your audience.
- Make eye contact with your audience. Include the whole group. Focus on one person at a time for three to four seconds each.
- Allow time for comments and questions if suitable for the occasion.
- Do not get defensive when asked questions; they are not personal attacks against you. Someone may not have understood something you said or may have a pertinent question.

12

Assessing Your Image

It is impossible to grow as a person if all efforts are focused on developing and enhancing physical appearance. No one can be fully attractive or whole unless there is a balance between inner and outer beauty.

Self-assessment

Before you can move forward in your life and fully develop, you must know where you have been, where you are now, and what you want to accomplish. Take time to make this assessment.

- Choose a quiet time of day.
- Choose a peaceful, serene setting.
- Relax your body and clear your mind for a few minutes.
- Be objective, fair, and honest in your self-evaluation.
- Do not be too easy on or overly critical of yourself.
- Make a list of your strengths.
- Make a list of your weaknesses.
- Decide what you want to change (and make a list of these decisions). Do not try to change everything at once!
- Be open to change.

Once you have evaluated your strengths and weaknesses, start to develop a plan of action. What image will be compatible with this?

Goals

Make a list of your goals. Choose what is important to you at this time. Decide when and how you would like to see these goals accomplished. Direction and discipline are equally important. Put this list in a place where you will see it easily and frequently. Do not be afraid to make changes to this list along the way if you feel the need to do so. Be committed to your goals and get started. Do not simply drift along and hope that everything will work out all right. You must trust your judgment and believe in your ability to accomplish your goals—*believe* that you can achieve these objectives.

Get started and have a sense of direction—do not try to accomplish everything overnight. Organize your plan of action. Be specific about how you intend to accomplish your goals, and always remember that a regular routine is easiest to follow. Be accepting of situations in your life that you cannot control.

Decide which goals you want to accomplish first, and remember that some goals are accomplished more realistically in stages. Set your priorities and be realistic in your timetable for reaching these goals. Do not put yourself under a lot of stress by being unrealistic. You are neither too young nor too old to pursue what you want in life. However, you must first accept yourself as you are now and feel confident that you are fine the way you are right now. You are on the way to making positive changes in your life.

Once you have committed yourself to change, do not allow yourself to be sidetracked by other people. You have to make up your own mind and decide what is best for you. Give yourself credit for changes or accomplishments as they occur—maybe even provide yourself with little treats along the way, like a new tie, shirt, or blouse, or perhaps some flowers or a special evening out. Use positive affirmations instead of constant self-criticism. Think positive thoughts and expect positive results.

Make a list of affirmations that support what you want to accomplish. Read them over frequently. While it is important to be open to success, do not be too hard on yourself if you do not accomplish your goals according to your projected timetable; it is possible to experience setbacks. Do not compare your progress to someone else's—your timetable for success is personal and individual. Remind yourself of your past accomplishments and draw strength from this.

Allow yourself to be open to success. If you always seem to be busy, but never actually accomplish anything, you need to examine this situation. Examine your behavior patterns, and recognize and confront any self-destructive behavior. If it is something that you cannot understand or seem to be able to change, perhaps joining a support group would be helpful. Otherwise, you will be continually frustrated. Remember, you can accomplish your goals: You are in the driver's seat of your own life, and it is important to give yourself permission to enact change. You are in control. You deserve success.

13

You, Irresistible You

Remember to allow some time to honor who you really are at the very core of your being. Let your uniqueness and individuality shine through.

Self-esteem and Attitude

Self-esteem is the value that you place on yourself. It is your sense of what you believe about yourself. You can make all kinds of things happen in your life—good or bad—depending on this belief. Positive self-esteem leads to self-appreciation and self-confidence. Your attitude expresses how you think, feel, and act.

When you are at peace with yourself and feel balanced within, this radiates outward in the form of a warm, genuine smile and sincere goodwill toward others. There will be a glow about you that acts like a magnet, pulling others to you—a charm both indescribable and irresistible!

Be yourself. Accept and love yourself for who you are right now. Start the day with a positive statement about yourself. Give yourself a quick pep talk: Tell yourself that you are lovable and wonderful just as you are right now, and hold that same thought for other people. Decide to join forces with other positive-thinking people when you get up in the morning.

You have to think highly of yourself before you can expect others to do so. Also, learn to laugh at yourself. A stoic, grim, or sour expression is a turn-off for the hardiest of souls. Keep your sense of humor! Having faith and confidence in yourself is very important. You can accomplish anything if you want it enough.

> *When Alice was in high school, she was preparing to go to the prom, which is a very special time. Alice was one of seven children, and her parents could not afford to buy her a gown. She would go to department stores and look at the beautiful displays of the gowns, knowing full well that she would not be able to afford one of them. Alice thought, "What shall I do? I won't allow myself to be defeated."*
>
> *Her father did some work in the next town for a woman who had two daughters who were about her age and size. From time to time she would send clothes home for Alice and they were a great fit. On one occasion she sent two gowns that*

belonged to her daughters. Alice thought that she could do something creative with one of these gowns. Perhaps she could have it cleaned and add a little touch here or there and have a wonderful prom gown. Alice had the gown cleaned and much to her disappointment, the beautiful outer layer on it came out limp. She had to think about what to do next. However, Alice refused to be defeated. She won $10 in an essay contest. She used this money to buy some fabric that matched her gown and stitched it on by hand to make an overskirt for the gown. It made the gown look beautiful.

When Alice went to the prom that night, all the girls were wearing the beautiful gowns that she had seen in the department stores. Alice held her head very high and carried herself very proudly as if this was the most beautiful gown in the world—and to her, it was. The girls admired her gown. They said, "Where did you get that gown? Why didn't we see that?"

Alice pulled herself up a few inches taller and thought of saying that her gown came from Paris. Then she thought, "Well, I'll settle for New York." She told them, "My gown was sent to me from New York," which was very impressive to everyone in her very small town.

If you are going through a bad time in your life, spend some time focusing on others and what is going on around you. Volunteer to help in a tutoring program, or simply shop for a home-bound senior neighbor. You will feel so much better once you stop focusing on your own problems for a while and you will receive much more than you ever gave. You can also spend some time reading and improving yourself during this time.

How You Relate to Other People

Be aware that what you think of yourself is reflected in how you treat other people and how you relate to them. Before you can begin to like other people, you must first like and love yourself. Accept other people as they are. Be interested in what is going on around you and in the lives of other people. The more interested you are in other people and other things, the more interesting you will be to other people. The more you are able to appreciate different points of view and ideas, other people and other cultures, the more other people will appreciate you. You will also be less self-conscious and less focused on yourself. As you know from previous experiences, it is both unattractive and boring to spend time with someone who is selfish and totally self-absorbed. Such a person appears vacant and totally lacking in charm, no matter how beautiful or handsome on the outside.

Be a good listener, and be sincere in your interest in other people. See the good in people and situations. Express your hope for others to succeed and wish them well. When you send positive thoughts to others or show your appreciation in small ways, it will always come back to you in some form. It often comes in unexpected ways. It is impossible to extend a kindness to someone else, no matter how small, without it somehow returning to you. The need for praise, appreciation, and recognition is universal—take the initiative in expressing this to others.

Appreciation can take many forms: a simple thank you, a pleasant smile, or a word of encouragement. Allow yourself the pleasure of doing something for someone else and do it without looking for something in return—it doesn't take a lot to make people feel special or valued.

When Liana was in college she met a student whose name was Marie. Marie was a wonderful person and Liana still thinks about her from time to time. Liana was not one of the most popular students in college. She didn't have beautiful clothes or much money. However, whenever Marie saw Liana she would speak to Liana as if Liana were the most popular person in the school. Marie was that way with everyone; she had a way of making someone feel as if he or she were the most special person in the world and just the person she wanted to see. Marie had a knack for making everyone feel special, whether it was the homecoming queen, the football players or one of the unpopular students like Liana. She made everyone feel special.

Your positive attitude will be reflected in the small, polite acts you are able to extend to others. Little courtesies and considerations are due everyone, regardless of personal opinions of them or whether they are worth impressing. It is very sad to see a person belittle or humiliate someone who is not in a position to fight back; it is the instigator, not the victim, who suffers the greatest loss. Nothing is sadder to see than someone who looks like a million dollars, who seems to have everything in life, but who has a negative attitude about everything and who dumps on helpless people.

Choosing Friends and Associates

Be responsible to yourself in your choice of associates and friends when possible. Eliminate people from your life who are constantly criticizing you or putting you down—you do not need these negative associations. Associate yourself with people who are rooting for you, people who are positive and enthusiastic, people who appreciate and are supportive of what you are trying to do. Do not let other people attempt to make you into something that you are not or do not want to be, and do not turn yourself into a lump of clay whose values or sense of self-worth changes in each pair of hands.

Avoid blaming others for what happens to you or for your shortcomings. Nothing can happen to you without your permission. Do not blame yourself for other people's shortcomings either. Do not allow yourself to be pulled into antagonistic situations or to be baited into becoming angry or falling apart emotionally. No one can hurt you with words or reject you *unless you give them permission to do so.*

If someone attempts to slight or ignore you or is prejudiced against you because of your race, religion, sex, age, beliefs or some personal quirk, do not feel bad. Drop them! Seek out more positive people in your life. Learn to be flexible. Things are not always going to go your way or as planned. Do not take this disappointment out on other people. Allow plenty of room for alternatives and changes in situations when relating to other people.

Criticizing Others

Criticism can be deeply hurtful and can be the final straw that breaks a person who is already badly damaged. Criticism should have a positive outcome—it is designed to bring about positive changes and it should be handled in a sensitive manner. Criticism does not have to be cruel; it should be justified, and only one criticism should be made at a time. Criticism should always be done privately. There is no need to humiliate someone, even if the criticism is justified.

The person being criticized should have an opportunity to respond, and the person who is criticizing should keep an open mind. The flip side of criticism, however, is praise and compliments. Be willing to give genuine praise generously whenever it is suitable or warranted.

Gossip

Gossip is a big no-no. While people will listen to someone criticize or stretch the truth about someone else, it will not really be appreciated. While it may hold their attention, that person will not be respected for doing so. People will wonder what is being said about *them* in their absence. A lack of trust will develop. It can also cause irreversible damage to a person's reputation. Someone once told this wonderful folk tale:

> *There was a little boy in a small town who loved to gossip. He enjoyed telling all kinds of fibs and half-truths about everyone. Sometimes people were seriously hurt by these stories. He began to feel a little badly about what he had done. He went to the town leader and confessed that he had told many half-truths. The boy asked him, "What should I do to make things all right?"*

The town leader thought a minute, and then he said, "Take two pillows full of feathers, go to the town square, spread the feathers all out and just let the wind take them wherever they land."

The boy did as he was told but he didn't feel any better. He watched the feathers float in all directions. He went back to the town leader and told him what he had done.

He said, "I don't feel any better. I still feel very sorry for what I have done."

The town leader told him, "Do this. Go and take the pillow cases that the feathers were in and put the feathers back into the pillow cases."

The boy went off in every direction trying to gather up these feathers. After trying for many hours, he had only a handful of feathers to show for his efforts. He went back to the town leader, discouraged and disappointed.

"Oh," he said to the town leader. "It was easy enough to let the feathers out of the pillows. But it was very hard to get the feathers back into them."

"I wasn't able to do it—they were scattered in all directions," he added.

The town leader looked at him and said, "That's the way it is with gossip. Once you say something about someone—something hurtful or untrue—it is scattered to the four winds, and you can never take it back."

Win-win Situations

Nothing should ever be gained at the expense of someone else. There is a great price to be paid for outwitting or outsmarting someone who is less capable in order to win or succeed at any cost. Life should be a win-win situation for everyone. Other people might not know what has happened, but it makes a person smaller for taking advantage of someone else—what you give in life is what you receive. When you root for other people to succeed, there are other people out there rooting for you, too.

Envy and Jealousy

When relating to other people, remember that you are never in competition with anyone else. You are unique; no one will ever do things quite the same way you do. Besides, there is plenty in life for everyone. You need never covet what someone else has. Avoid being envious or jealous of someone else's new job, promotion, or wonderful friendship—the same is also available to you. When you understand this, you need never again feel threatened by anyone else. The sky is the limit for you. You can have it all! No one can stand in your way or thwart your endeavors without your consent.

Hatred and Bitterness

Feelings of hatred and bitterness destroy the soul and block the flow of positive energy. These negative feelings can put a person out of balance with life. They prevent intended goodness from traveling to that person, and they will affect the way that someone looks and feels. Negative feelings become etched on the face, and when this happens, a person can definitely be less attractive.

You Can Make a Difference

You should never assume that things are always going well for someone else or make assumptions about other people in general—good or bad. You never know how much the person next to you at work or lunch is hurting, in spite of appearance. The beautiful office manager who appears to have everything may be going through a really tough time; a warm smile or a word of kindness can make all the difference in the world to her on a particular day. You can make a difference in people's lives on any given day, often in little ways. Step out of your own problems and think about other people. If you are considerate of others, and project warmth and sincerity as well as genuine interest, this will enhance anything else that you have to offer.

Victimization

If you have grown up as a victim of any kind of abuse—mental, spiritual, emotional or physical—strive to put it behind you. You deserve to be free! Do not unconsciously seek out situations that perpetuate this vicious cycle. Placing blame on yourself will ensure that you continue to act like a victim. Allow yourself to heal; seek professional help or join a support group. You must learn to forgive yourself for things over which you have had no control.

14

Tap into Your Golden Treasures

When all is said and done, you are irresistible right here and right now just as you are. The more you accept this truth, the more irresistible you will become as you allow yourself to appreciate and accept yourself.

A Smile Can Warm the Coolest Heart

This is your most appealing asset. When all else fails, a genuine smile can work wonders. It can be a real icebreaker and can help someone else to relax. You will find yourself in situations that will be awkward, and no words will seem appropriate. You may meet someone who seems cold and distant, haughty, and unreachable. In reality, this person may be very insecure; a smile may be just what that person needs at the moment. Only the coldest of hearts can refuse to return an honest smile.

Laughter Is the Best Medicine

Laughter can be a real icebreaker. It is no accident (or small feat) that some of the greatest public speakers today have a real talent for eliciting laughter from their audiences.

Laughter has a way of putting people at ease and helping them take themselves less seriously. Laughter can relieve tension in the body and ease stress. Life has its serious side, and laughter is needed to give life balance.

If you are feeling tense or strained, look in your mirror and give yourself permission to laugh for a full minute: You will feel wonderful. You can also make laughter a part of your regular exercise or fitness program, or you can include a full minute of laughter in your work-out routine. It will work wonders for you.

A Sense of Humor Can Lighten a Difficult Moment

There are occasions or situations in life that you cannot control. You can do one of several things in response: scream, bang your head against a wall, or accept the situation at hand. At times like these, it can be helpful to look for the lighter side of the situation. Granted, it might take a little digging to find it, but when all else fails, it's worth trying.

Humor can also keep you from taking yourself too seriously, which puts you under a lot of pressure. It lets you know that you can go on by keeping things in perspective.

Inner Joy and Happiness Are Contagious

There is something about inner joy and happiness that refuses to be contained. They have a way of bubbling over with or without your permission. When this happens, it is impossible for others around you to not be affected or drawn to you. They have a magnetic and wondrous appeal.

Humility and Compassion Sweeten the Heart

A well-rounded person will always have these personality aspects. They give balance to the heart and a sense of empathy. These are traits (characteristics) that the most successful people possess. There is no need to publicly advertise them; they are an integral part of that person—just like an arm, a leg or a tooth.

Gratitude Attracts its Own Reward

Be grateful for all that you have received. Takers in life never pause to reflect on what they already have. When you are grateful for what you have been given, the door is opened for you to receive even more.

Forgiveness Opens the Door to Freedom

It's been said that forgiveness is a gift that you give yourself. This might sound like a contradiction, but it really is true. Often grudges are held against people who are not aware of these feelings or who simply do not care. It is better to let them go rather than let them eat away at your soul. This frees up space for wonderful, positive things to come into your life. If you are having trouble letting go, then seek professional counseling. It is worth it.

Appreciation and Respect Are Great Motivators

Everyone wants to feel appreciated and respected. The value of a well-earned compliment or the acknowledgement for a job well done is priceless. When someone is appreciated and given well-earned respect, that person will often be more motivated and loyal to you in a way that no amount of money can purchase. By the same token, people who are rude and unappreciative and place little value on someone can pay no amount of money for loyalty or respect.

Love Is the Ultimate Gift

It can light up a face or the world. Love warms and dazzles the heart in a way that diamonds never can.

Part III

Think Success

15

Thoughts Are Powerful

Think success. Thoughts affect every part of your life. They are at the core of your short-term and long-term success or failure. Get your day off to a successful start with winning thoughts and affirmations . . .

1. Today I smile at the world, and the world smiles back at me.

2. My thoughts are magnetic. They attract similar thoughts. Today, I send out thoughts that are loving and beautiful.

3. Today is one of a kind. No day will ever be quite the same. It is mine to use exactly as I like. What a glorious gift!

4. Wherever I go, I leave trails of happiness and joy, sprinkled with good will and blessings.

5. Life offers me anything that I can accept. I accept success, love, joy, health, and prosperity wrapped in humility and gratitude.

6. I am kind and loving to myself. Therefore, I can be kind and loving to others.

7. The more I love and accept myself, the more love I have to give and share with others.

8. I can never receive more in life than I give. What I get out of life today will be directly in proportion to what I give.

9. I am in control of my day. I take responsibility for my day. This starts with taking control of my thoughts.

10. My level of success in any area is directly proportional to my level of self-esteem.

11. I attract as much success and prosperity as I can accept.

12. Today I find a reason to laugh, even if it means laughing at myself.

These affirmations are designed to give you ongoing support and encouragement when you need it. You can cut them out and carry them with you, or place them in areas that can be easily seen.

Today,
I smile at the world,
and the world
smiles back at me.

My thoughts are magnetic. They attract similar thoughts. Today, I send out thoughts that are loving and beautiful.

Today is one of a kind.
No day will ever be
quite the same.
It is mine to use
exactly as I like.
What a glorious gift!

Wherever I go,
I leave trails of
happiness and joy,
sprinkled with
good will and blessings.

Life offers me anything that I can accept. I accept success, love, joy, health, and prosperity wrapped in humility and gratitude.

I am kind and loving
to myself.
Therefore, I can be
kind and loving to others.

The more that I love and accept myself, the more love I have to give and share with others.

I can never receive more in life than I give. What I get out of life today will be directly proportional to what I give.

I am in control of my day.
I take responsibility
for my day.
This starts with taking
control of my thoughts.

My level of success in any area is directly in proportion to my level of self-esteem.

I attract as much success and prosperity as I can accept.

Today,
I find a reason to laugh,
even if it means laughing
at myself.

Remember, you are special and unique. Personalize the information in this book to unlock the door to your own personal, professional, and financial success. Make your 30 seconds count!

Index